RUDOLF STEINER
An Illustrated Biography

D0896225

RUDOLF STEINER
An Illustrated Biography

Johannes Hemleben

SOPHIA BOOKS

Sophia Books
Hillside House, The Square,
Forest Row, E. Sussex
RH18 5ES

www.rudolfsteinerpress.com

Published by Sophia Books 2000
An imprint of Rudolf Steiner Press

Reprinted 2010

First published in English by Henry Goulden Ltd. 1975
Translated by Leo Twyman
Originally published in German by Rowohlt Taschenbuch Verlag 1963

A catalogue record for this book is available from the British Library

ISBN 978 1 85584 093 5

Cover by Andrew Morgan Design
Typeset by DP Photosetting, Aylesbury, Bucks
Printed and bound in Great Britain by Cpod, Trowbridge, Wilts

CONTENTS

Contents

PREFACE

Immortal—as yet unborn—only one who understands both
these states will understand eternity.

Rudolf Steiner

Rudolf Steiner's *Autobiography**, most of which he dictated
from his sickbed in the last months of his life, under the title
of *Mein Lebensgang*, has surprisingly little to say about the
private side of his life. All the more care, however, does he
devote to the account of the objective development of his
striving for knowledge, starting from the early awakening of
his interest in geometry and Copernicanism, passing on to the
study of Kant, and ending with his experience of the meditative life as a fully mature man. He believed that it was
presumptuous, and not to the purpose, to give an account of
his private and personal experiences.

> For it was my constant endeavour to present what I had to say,
> and what I believed I should do, in such a way as to stress
> objective rather than personal aspects. While I have always
> believed that in many fields it is the personality that most gives
> colour and substance to human activities, still it appears to me
> that this personal element must find expression in speech and
> action, not through the contemplation of one's own person-
> ality. Whatever may emerge from this contemplation is a
> matter about which an individual has to come to an under-
> standing with himself.

Steiner's reticence about his personal experience serves to
bring into sharper focus the objective circumstances of his life.

---

* *Autobiography. Chapters from the Course of my Life*, Anthroposophic
Press, Hudson, 2000.

CHILDHOOD AND YOUTH

Rudolf Steiner was born at the frontier between central and eastern Europe. He himself looked upon it as something more than chance that he should have been born there. His birth to Austrian parents at Kraljevec (which is now in Croatia but was then in Hungary near its border with the Austrian empire) assumed for him symbolic significance. This east-west polarity held him in a state of tension which was to remain with him throughout his life.

'Both my father and my mother were true children of the glorious forestlands of Lower Austria, north of the Danube.' Right up to our time, this remote region has remained to a great extent shielded from the destructive influences of civilization. Here his father was employed as a gamekeeper

Rudolf Steiner's mother:
Franziska Steiner, née Blie
(1834–1918)

in the service of a count. The desire to establish a family led him to change his occupation.

> So he gave up his post as gamekeeper and became a tele-graphist on the Austrian railway. His first post was at a small station in southern Styria. Next he was transferred to Kralje-vec on the Hungarian–Croatian border. It was at this time that he married my mother. Her maiden name is Blie. She comes of an old-established family of Horn. I was born at Kraljevec on 27 February 1861—So it comes about that my birthplace is far distant from the corner of the earth to which I rightly belong.

Two days after his birth Rudolf Steiner received Roman Catholic baptism in the neighbouring village.

The child remained in Kraljevec for only one and a half years. After six months in Mödling near Vienna his father was transferred once more, this time to Pottschach station on the Semmering line—which for those days was a technolo-

His father: Johann Steiner (1829–1910)

gical marvel. This was where the boy spent his childhood from his second to his eighth year. To the end of his life Rudolf Steiner looked to that period with joy and gratitude.

> The scenes amidst which I passed my childhood were marvellous. The prospect embraced the mountains linking Lower Austria with Styria: Schneeberg, Wechsel, Raxalpe, Semmering. The bald rockface of the Schneeberg caught the sun's rays, which, when they were projected on to the little station on fine summer days, were the first intimation of the dawn. The grey ridge of the Wechsel made a sombre contrast.
>
> The green prospects which welcomed the observer on every side made it seem as if the mountains were thrusting upwards of their own volition. The majestic peaks filled the distance, and the charm of nature lay all around.

In these words Rudolf Steiner describes the natural scenes that he knew in his childhood. Against this has to be set the

Rudolf Steiner's birthplace at Kraljevec

fact that the milieu in which he grew up was largely the product of his father's occupation. The family, to which in course of time a brother and a sister were added, lived in the station house, directly in front of which ran the railway track. The arrival and departure of the trains, the ringing of the signals, the mechanical rattle of the telegraph, created the atmosphere and divided up the day.

At that time, of course, trains were few and far between in this part of the world; but when they did come, usually there were some of the village folk who had time on their hands assembled at the station, looking for diversion in a life which

Pottschach station

otherwise they apparently found too monotonous. The schoolmaster, the parson, the steward of the estate, and often the mayor, put in an appearance.

The arrival, say, of a certain train from Vienna was the daily event that drew the leading lights together and stirred the children into activity.

It was against this background that from his earliest years the young Rudolf Steiner became aware of the polarity of nature and technology. He experienced the healing virtues of unspoilt nature, and at the same time felt the attraction of the growing power of technology.

> I believe that my childhood in such an environment was an important influence on my life. For the mechanical aspects of this life engaged my interest in a compelling manner. And I am aware of how again and again these interests cast a shadow over the emotive side of my childish being, which was drawn towards nature, at once so gracious and so vast, into which, for all their enslavement to the mechanical arts, these railway trains always vanished.

Two further childhood influences were school and church, the schoolmaster and the parson. After a difference of opinion with the village schoolmaster, who it seems was none too competent, his father took on the task of educating the young Steiner.

'And so for hours together I sat beside him at his desk, where I was supposed to write and read while he proceeded with his duties.' Not surprisingly, nothing much came of this. The boy gave much more attention to what was going on on the railway than to the toil demanded by his first attempts at writing. He was interested in handling the pounce box and sharpening the quills—less so in the beauty of the letters he had formed. But he also retained in his memory one human figure. The priest from the neighbouring village of St

Valentin visited the Steiner family almost daily. He was an eccentric, and at the same time 'representative of the liberal catholic clergy, tolerant and affable. He was witty, liked cracking jokes, and enjoyed seeing people laugh'. He was knowledgeable on the subject of dumplings and baking recipes. He was caustically critical of the institutions of his own church, so that he radiated an atmosphere in which the traditional religious attitudes melted away. But his criticism was tinged with humour, without fanatical bitterness, and he left the traditional forms of the church to do their work. Zeal for reform was far from the mind of this lovable Austrian.

Neudörfl

When the boy was coming up to eight, the Steiner family moved from Pottschach to Neudörfl, a small Hungarian village an hour's journey from Wiener-Neustadt. This move brought the young Rudolf Steiner considerably closer to modern civilization. The Alps, and the wooded landscape which lay before them, once so near and so dear to him, withdrew into the distance and were now no more than the backdrop on the horizon. The Rosalien-Gebirge, on whose slopes Neudörfl lies, was a reminder of the wooded paradise that he had lost. This range of wooded hills lies, a kindly, sheltering screen, before one comes to Hungary and its wide steppes.

Seen from the top of the Rosalien-Gebirge, the Vienna basin extends in a wide vista, in the foreground of which can be seen the industrial centre of Wiener-Neustadt, not very large but humming with intense activity.

To the growing boy these woods were a blessing.

For in the woods there were blackberries, raspberries, and strawberries. Often it gave one a sense of deep satisfaction to spend an hour and a half gathering a contribution to the family's evening meal, which otherwise would have consisted merely of a slice of bread and butter or bread and cheese for each.

Half-an-hour on foot from Neudörfl is Sauerbrunn, where there is a spring with carbonated chalybeate mineral water. The road to it follows the railway, part of the way through

The region in which Rudolf Steiner spent his youth

beautiful woods. In the school holidays I used to go there early every morning, carrying a *Blutzer*. This is a clay water pitcher. Mine held about 3 to 4 litres. There was no charge for filling it at the spring. The family drank the pleasant-tasting, sparkling water at the midday meal.

Clearly, Rudolf Steiner grew up in simple circumstances— austere and healthy. There is no hint in his boyhood of any softening or pampering influences. He describes the economic situation of his parents as a 'struggle against the poor wages of such minor railway officials', adding that they 'were always willing to spend their last coppers on whatever would benefit their children, but there were not many of these last coppers to be had'.

At Neudörfl the boy attended the village school in the main street of the village. With its low houses and broad layout, it made a strikingly oriental impression.

The school at Neudörfl

Between the two rows of houses flowed a brook, and to the sides of the houses were magnificent nut-trees. In relation to these nut-trees the schoolchildren had worked out an order of precedence amongst themselves. When the nuts began to ripen, the boys and girls bombarded the trees with stones and this way gathered a winter store of nuts. In autumn, the talk was almost entirely about the size of the nut harvest each one had gathered. He who had gathered the most was the one most looked up to. The others followed in order of precedence— and last of all came myself, who, as a 'foreigner', was not entitled to a place in this order at all.

The railway station, which at the same time was the home of the Steiner family, stands above the village. The church with its surrounding graveyard is halfway up the hill, so that

The Neudörfl station building

the boy passed the church on his way to school every day. There was an equally close inner relationship between the church and the school. Everything that happened in the school was interrelated with the church. In a single schoolroom, five classes of boys and girls were taught simultaneously, in the way that was customary in village schools in those days. The schoolmaster only seldom made an appearance. His main occupation was as village notary, and he had an assistant master to represent him. In his possession the boy found a geometry book. This was one of the decisive moments of his youth.

> I tackled it with enthusiasm. For weeks my mind was full of congruence, the similarity of triangles, quadrangles, polygons; I racked my brains over the problem of where the parallel lines really meet; Pythagoras' theorem fascinated me. To be able to grasp something purely in my mind brought me inner happiness. *I know that it was in the study of geometry that I first found happiness.*

It may seem hardly credible that a boy no more than nine years old should be capable of such experiences. But they are typical of Rudolf Steiner, and tell us a great deal about him. There are instances of them throughout his development.

> As a child I felt, without of course expressing it to myself clearly, that knowledge of the spiritual world is something to be grasped in the mind in the same way as geometrical concepts. For I was as certain of the reality of the spiritual world as of the physical world. But I needed in some way to justify this assumption. I needed to be able to tell myself that experience of the spiritual world is no more an illusion than knowledge of the physical world. I told myself that geometry was something that only the mind by the exercise of its own powers could grasp; this feeling was my justification for speaking of the spiritual world that I experienced in the same way as I did of

the physical world. And that was how I spoke of it. There were two concepts which, though vague, had already become an important part of my mental life before I was eight years old. I distinguished things and essences that 'one saw' from those that 'one did not see'.

He comforted himself with the certainty that there are realities that are invisible. This experience was the light without which he would have remained only dimly aware of the physical world. 'With his geometry book, the assistant master at Neudörfl gave me the justification I needed at that time for my view of the spiritual world.'

Further, this assistant master awakened in him an interest in the arts.

He played the violin and the piano. And he drew a great deal. Both these accomplishments attracted me towards him. At the age of no more than nine, he had me making charcoal drawings.

The assistant master was also church organist and custodian of the vestments and the other church ornaments and utensils; he assisted the priest in everything connected with the administration of the rites. We schoolboys served at the altar and sang in the choir at masses, requiems, and funerals. My boyish mind was attuned to the solemn Latin and the church ceremonial. Through my active participation in church affairs up to the age of ten I was often in the company of the priest, whom I esteemed very highly.

Reflecting on my boyhood at Neudörfl, I was struck by the way in which the combination of church ceremony and sacred music compellingly evokes for our contemplation the enigmas of existence. The study of the bible, and the teaching of the catechism by the priest made less of an impression on my mind than his performance of the rites as mediator between the natural and the supernatural world. From the very beginning this was to me no mere form, but a profound experience, the

Rudolf Steiner served as an altar boy in the church at Neudörfl

more so as in this respect I stood alone at home, in my parents' house.

At home there was nothing to foster my relationship with the church. My father took no interest in it. At that time he was a 'free-thinker'.

The fact that his father was a 'free-thinker' did not prevent the boy from receiving confirmation.

Opposite the school was the presbytery. Here lived the priest, who was responsible for the supervision of the lessons and who also gave religious instruction twice a week.

The image of this man is deeply engraved in my mind.... Of the people I had got to know up to my tenth or eleventh year, he was by far the most significant.

Moreover, it is to this priest that I owe in very great measure the intellectual leanings that I developed later, and *one* powerful impression especially remains with me. One day he came into the school, assembled the 'more mature' pupils, in whose number he included me, in the little master's study, unfolded a drawing he had made, and explained the Copernican system to us with reference to it. He was very clear on the subject of the earth's movement round the sun, the rotation of the axis, the inclined axis of the earth, summer and winter, and the zones of the earth. I found the subject quite absorbing, spent days making drawings to illustrate it, then received further special instruction from the priest about eclipses of the sun and moon, and from then on concentrated all my intellectual curiosity on the subject.

Wiener-Neustadt

From the age of eleven Steiner attended the modern school (Realschule) in neighbouring Wiener-Neustadt. He now had to travel to school every day by railway. But it was often impossible to make the journey because the line was out of operation or because the connections were bad. The journey then had to be made on foot. Neudörfl was in Hungary, Wiener-Neustadt in Lower Austria. Between them flowed the Leitha, the river that marked the border. So every day Rudolf Steiner had to cross from Hungary to Austria and back. In fine weather this meant one hour's travel. But in winter the railway and footpath were often completely snowed up. Then the boy would have to make his way laboriously through knee-deep snow. Sometimes his sister would meet him at the outskirts of the village and relieve him of his heavy school satchel. In old age he did not regret the heavy demands made on his physical strength in his youth. He believed that it was to this that he owed his good health later in life. Town life faced him with problems. However close he felt to life in the woods and fields, however secure he felt in the realm of mathematics and pure speculation, in the external world, in the bustle of the city streets, he stood helpless. 'I stood bemused, wondering what was going on in the houses that stood row upon row.' This problem of achieving the same rapport with town life as with his inner world was to exercise him for the next two decades.

The subject that made most impression on him at the modern school was mathematics. He came into possession of an essay by his headmaster (Heinrich Schramm) in a school report, entitled 'The force of attraction considered as an effect of movement'. Of course he was without the acquired knowledge which he needed in order to understand a work the chief basis of which was integral calculus. Unflagging effort, combined with the ordinary school lessons, enabled him within a short time to overcome this difficulty. There were two teachers who gave him considerable help in his pursuit of these studies: Laurenz Jelinek, physicist and mathematician, and Georg Kosak, teacher of geometry. Through guidance, and through studying assiduously on his own, this boy of twelve or thirteen years acquired considerable knowledge of descriptive geometry and of probability calculus. He himself speaks of his 'infatuation with geometry' at this time.

Kosak was for him a teacher

> who truly embodied the ideal that my mind suggested to me. He was one whom I could seek to emulate. His method of instruction was extremely systematic and clear. Starting from the principles, he built up the argument with such clarity that in following him the capacity for thinking derived the utmost benefit.

Steiner's abilities did not go unrecognized by the school authorities, so that

The modern school—Realschule—at Wiener-Neustadt

from the fourth class onwards he received a mark for descriptive geometry and drawing that was never otherwise awarded. The highest commendation, which was very hard to achieve, was 'excellent'—he was commended as 'outstanding'.

It may truly be asserted without boasting that at sixteen or seventeen the boy had progressed to a point where he had absorbed such of the works of Kant as had been published by the Reclamsche Universal-Bibliothek.

The study of philosophy opened up a new world for him.

This was the time when the Reclamsche Universal-Bibliothek was for the first time bringing out popular editions of learned works which had hitherto been inaccessible to the public at large. In his straitened financial circumstances, this was a great boon to the intellectual aspirations of young Rudolf Steiner. Thus, when no more than fourteen years of

age he was able to acquire Kant's *Critique of Pure Reason*.
Because his teacher's history lessons bored him and he
needed his free time for his homework, he took his school
history book apart and 'pasted neatly between its pages those
of Kant's *Critique of Pure Reason*'. And so during school
lessons he industriously and thoroughly studied the works of
Kant.

At the same time this boy, who was trained to think with
mathematical clarity and for whom well-ordered, lucid
thoughts were a condition of his very existence, 'was seeking
to reconcile this brand of thinking with religious dogma'.
Because he never had the least reason to doubt the existence
and effectual working of a spiritual world, he lived without
opposition and with true devotion to the dogmas of the
church, knowledge of which was available to him through
good textbooks on dogma, symbolism, and ecclesiastical
history.

For self-evident reasons, in order 'to contribute at least a
little of what my parents had to pay out of their meagre
income for my schooling', from the age of fifteen onwards
Rudolf Steiner gave private tuition, 'either to fellow pupils in
the same year as himself, or to pupils in a lower class. I owe a
great deal to this tuition work'.

But this was not all. Because his father wished him to
become an engineer, he had attended a modern school
(Realschule) and not a grammar school (Gymnasium) and so
lacked any knowledge of the classical languages. He found
this a grievous deprivation. 'And so I bought myself Latin
and Greek textbooks and quite secretly pursued a course of
private classical studies in addition to my modern education.'
Later, as a student, he was able, thanks to this self-study, to
coach grammar-school boys in the classical languages.

In 1879, at the age of eighteen, he passed his school-leaving
examination. His school-leaving certificate is still kept at the

school. It reads: 'Entry in respect of school-leaver Steiner, Rudolf, from Kraljevec in Hungary, born 27 February 1861, son of Johann Steiner, station master at Neudörfl on the Südbahn, catholic, commenced his schooling in school year 1872/3 at the modern school at Wiener-Neustadt and completed it in all classes in the school year 1878/79. His behaviour was exemplary. His report reads: "Passed with distinction".'

Vienna

In order that his son could study at the Vienna Polytechnic, the elder Steiner had arranged for a transfer from Neudörfl to Inzersdorf near Vienna.

This can hardly have meant an advancement in his career. As regards the environment it was a change very much for the worse. It would be hard to find a more desolate spot in

Rudolf Steiner as a pupil in his school-leaving year. Wiener-Neustadt, 1879

the whole of Austria. 'The station was far from the village, solitary in a landscape without charm.' Today, sidings and a repair workshop are features of the scene. Gone are the woodland paradises of Pottschach and the Rosalien-Gebirge. But the opportunities for study are there. In the autumn of 1879 Rudolf Steiner entered the Technical University of Vienna. He read biology, chemistry, physics, and mathematics. It seemed as if his father's dream that he should become an engineer was to come true. But the reality was to be otherwise.

Between passing out of school and commencing his advanced studies Rudolf Steiner, by selling his school books, had been able to acquire a number of works of the great philosophers of German idealism. From Kant and his painstakingly evolved theory of knowledge he now turned his attention to Fichte, Hegel, Schelling, and their pupils, and already even to Darwin.

Fichte's 'philosophy of the Ego' is the one great human theme whose echoes resound throughout the nineteenth and twentieth centuries. Kierkegaard, Stirner, Nietzsche, took up this theme and made their response to it without achieving any general measure of agreement. 'The destiny of Man', his self-determination and his dependence on the universe, is here the question that is insistently raised. Man's Ego, the spiritual core of his being, puts him in a special category in relation to all other forms of existence. What is his mission, what part is he to play in the natural order of things? These are the questions which Rudolf Steiner confronted round about his twentieth year.

My preoccupation with the concepts of natural science had led me finally to a position in which I saw the activity of the human Ego as the only possible point from which to advance towards true knowledge. I put it to myself that when the Ego is in

action and contemplates its own activity, then a spiritual entity
is directly present in the consciousness.

In order to come to a clearer understanding of his own
intellectual position and to define the points at which he
agreed with and differed from Fichte's theory of knowledge,
he took it a page at a time 'and rewrote it'.

> Before, I had cudgelled my brains in an attempt to find con-
> cepts for natural phenomena and on the basis of them to
> develop a concept for the Ego. I now proposed to reverse this
> procedure and, starting from the Ego, to penetrate into the
> workings of nature. At that time I saw spirit and nature as two
> quite distinct opposites. For me, a world of spiritual entities
> existed. It was by direct perception that I was aware that the
> Ego, itself spirit, exists in a spiritual world. *But there was no
> place for nature in the spiritual world of my experience.*

In this confession, Rudolf Steiner once again touches on
the cardinal point of his own spiritual development. In this,
unlike modern man, to him the world of spirit is not a problem, a country to which entry is barred. For him, the riddle
whose solution was fraught with difficulties was the natural
world, and how to live in it.

Even in childhood Steiner had displayed powers of clairvoyance which left him in no doubt that 'behind' and 'above'
the world of the senses there is a spiritual world. Thus, from
early on the problem for him was, not: 'Is there a spiritual
world?' but: 'How are the physical world and the spiritual
world related to each other?'

> At that time I felt it my bounden duty to seek the truth
> through the medium of philosophy. I was committed to the
> study of mathematics and science. I was convinced that I
> could never stand in a proper relationship to them unless I
> could rest their results on a secure philosophical foundation.
> *But to me there was a spiritual world which was reality.* The

spiritual individuality of each and every person was revealed to me with the utmost clarity. The physical body, and activity in the physical world, were merely its revelation. It was united with what came as a physical embryo from the parents. I followed the man who had died into the spiritual world.

In the eighties of the nineteenth century, what path was a young man to follow who was aware that he possessed these faculties? Materialism had brought everything, even theology, under its sway. The experience of communion with the souls of the departed was in the eyes of his contemporaries nothing but hallucination, the evidence of a sick mind. A man who spoke of such experiences was certain to be received with derision and scorn. The best he could hope for was sympathy for a highly gifted young man whose mind, tragically, had become sick.

In a lecture he gave in Berlin in 1913 which he described as a thumbnail sketch for a biography, Rudolf Steiner related how this unusual faculty which he possessed for experiencing communion with the souls of the dead had been with him even as a child. It will have been about 1868, that is in his eighth year. He was sitting in the station waiting room at Pottschach. As he sat there, it seemed to him that the door opened and

> the figure of a woman came through the door, advanced to the middle of the room, made gestures, and spoke something like these words: Now and always, try to do for me whatever you can—then she stayed for a while, making gestures such as, once seen, can never be erased from the mind.

Then this female figure disappeared, and the boy was alone once more. The child knew that this was no human being in the physical sense. But how to cope with an experience of this nature?

There was no one in the family with whom he could have talked about such a thing, simply because if he had related this experience he would have been rebuked in the severest terms for his foolish superstitions.

Some days later it was learned that at the very time when the boy had had this experience in the waiting room a close relation had taken her own life in a place many miles away. There was no doubt in the boy's mind that he had seen the soul of the departed and that she had begged him for help in the future.

This experience made a powerful impression on him. But it was only the first instance of his faculty of natural clairvoyance, which remained with him throughout his life, and which, unusual though it was, became as it were a matter of course. The invisible was to him visible.

And from that time forth the boy lived with the spirits of nature, which are particularly to be observed in such surroundings, with the creative entities behind things, just as he lived with and was acted on by the external world.

But, as has been said, he was alone with his gift of natural, spontaneous clairvoyance. It is a sign of the soundness and firmness of his mind that he summoned up the power of silence and digested his experiences in the quietude of his own mind. If he had spent his childhood in the forests of Finland or in the Himalayas, his gift of second sight would probably not have been regarded as anything unusual. He would quite naturally have met with understanding from those around him. But in Central Europe as it was towards the end of the nineteenth century, in Central Europe which 100 years earlier had only slowly, almost with reluctance, come to recognize that Emmanuel Swedenborg possessed the gift of clairvoyance—see Kant's *Träume eines Geistersehers* (Dreams of a Visionary)—a young man who did not wish to become the laughing stock of those around him must hold his peace. He remained silent until a benevolent fate brought him the acquaintance of a man to whom he could speak of these things.

To reach Vienna, the eighteen-year-old student had to travel by railway from Inzersdorf to the Süd railway station.

And so it happened that I made the acquaintance of a simple man of the people. Every week he travelled to Vienna by the same train as me. He gathered medicinal herbs from the land and sold them to pharmacists in Vienna. We became friends. One could speak to him about the world of spirits as to someone who had had experience of it. He was intensely pious. He was without formal education. It is true that he had read a great many mystical works; but his reading in no way influenced what he said. The words that he spoke were the emanations of a mental life that bore the marks of elemental creative wisdom. In his company one was afforded a profound insight into the secrets of nature. On his back were his bundles of herbs; but in his heart was the knowledge of the spiritual aspects of nature that had come to him through his gathering of them. And so gradually I came to feel that I was in company with a soul from ancient times, who, untouched by civilization, science, or the contemplation of the present, brought close to me the intuitive knowledge of former times.

Of learning in the normally accepted sense of the term there was nothing to be gained from this man. But one who sensed the spiritual world in himself was able through the intermediary of another to gain a profound and lasting insight into it.

Rudolf Steiner never revealed the name of this herb-gatherer who meant so much to him in his spiritual solitude. Through the persistence of Emil Bock the mystery surrounding this simple man has now been dispelled. His name was Felix Koguzki. He was born in Vienna on 1 August 1833,

The herb-gatherer Felix Koguzki (1833–1909) with his wife and sons

and at the time that Rudolf Steiner knew him he was living at Trumau, a village to the south of Vienna, in extremely modest circumstances, though his life was well regulated. He died in 1909 and was buried in the cemetery at Trumau. His gravestone has been well looked after, and the inscription reads: 'Here lies Felix Koguzki, who departed this life in 1909, aged 76 years.'

In the Mystery Dramas which he wrote between 1910 and 1913, Rudolf Steiner immortalized this herb-gatherer under the name of Felix Balde.

There is another man whose name he never revealed. We know him only from occasional references by Steiner. He must have met this 'person unknown' in Vienna shortly after his first encounter with the herb-gatherer. This man referred him to certain significant passages in Fichte which pointed him in a direction that led him to produce, as it were from the seed, his *Outline of Esoteric Science* (formerly *Occult Science*).

And Fichte's tenets were the starting point of many of our
discussions at that time on the material from which *Occult
Science* developed. This excellent man's occupation was as
humble as that of Felix himself.

Rudolf Steiner told Edouard Schuré of this encounter when
he was his guest at Barr in Alsace in 1907.

In the preface to the French edition of Rudolf Steiner's
Christianity as Mystical Fact, Schuré wrote: 'The master
whom Rudolf Steiner met was one of those potent personalities who are on earth to fulfill a mission under the mask of
some homely occupation.... Anonymity is the essential
condition for their power, but only serves to make their
influence more lasting, for they arouse, teach, and guide
those who can do their work in full view of the world.' Rudolf
Steiner had already marked out his task for himself: To
reunite religion and science. To bring God into science and
nature into religion. From this position to revitalize art and
life.

But how was he to set about this unexampled and daring
mission? How was he to overcome or rather to tame and
convert, his great adversary, the spirit of the nineteenth
century? How was he to harness the dragon of modern natural science to the vehicle of spiritual knowledge? And above
all, how was he to overcome the bull of public opinion? To his
students' questions the 'Master' gave the characteristic reply:
'To overcome the enemy, you must begin by understanding
him. You can only become the conqueror of the dragon by
slipping into his skin.'

From the conversations that he had with Rudolf Steiner at
Barr, Schuré deduced that Rudolf Steiner's second 'helper'
was one of those persons who in the esoteric language of both
East and West have from time immemorial been known as
'Initiates'.

We cannot judge how close to historical fact Schuré's view comes. But at all events it does get to the heart of what Rudolf Steiner from his student years onwards had defined as his purpose. He told himself: If you wish to bring your own inner experience into harmony with the intellectual consciousness of your environment, so as to overcome effectively the constantly growing power of materialism as a world philosophy and a way of life, you must first assume the intellectual attitude of nineteenth century man. You must get inside the dragon's skin. Only when you have mastered the method of science and have perceived the limited extent to which the view of the world built up by science conveys the truth, will you be able to bring into operation in the West a spiritual philosophy of the world. For the young man, a long, wearisome road lay ahead.

Karl Julius Schröer

Steiner was greatly helped in the course of study that he now needed by becoming acquainted with his German teacher, Karl Julius Schröer, who lectured on German literature at the Vienna Polytechnic. In the winter semester of 1879/80 he lectured on: 'German Literature since Goethe and Schiller's Life and Works.'

> From the very first lecture I was enthralled. The ardour of his treatment, the inspiring way in which he read from the poets during the lectures, were an intensely stimulating introduction to poetry.

Now, at nineteen years of age, Steiner read Goethe's *Faust* for the first time, with avid interest.

> Then, after no more than a few lectures I became more closely acquainted with Schröer. He afterwards often took me home with him, added a word here and a word there to what he had

*Professor Karl Julius
Schröer (1825–1900)*

said in his lectures, readily answered my questions, and lent me books from his library to read when I left. On these occasions he let fall many a word about the second part of *Faust* which at the time he was busy editing and writing a commentary on. This too I read at that time.

I thank God and a happy fate that has brought me the acquaintance here in Vienna of a man whom I esteem and honour as teacher, scholar, poet, and man—Karl Julius Schröer.

So wrote the student Steiner to a friend on 13 January 1881. Schröer's central purpose was to root out from educated society the firmly entrenched error that the second part of *Faust* was a feeble product of Goethe's old age. Up to a point he may be said to have succeeded in his purpose. Schröer has another achievement to his credit, in that he rescued from oblivion the Oberufer Christmas Plays, which he published as

'German Christmas Plays from Hungary'. These were performed annually by German peasants who had emigrated to
the Bratislava region of Hungary. Later, by presenting them
regularly at the Goetheanum, Rudolf Steiner instilled new
life into them.

But it was on Goethe that Schröer chiefly focussed:

> When in his company, I warmed to him. I have sat at his side
> for hours at a time. At these times when I was alone with him I
> truly felt that there was a third person present: Goethe. For
> Schröer felt so intensely the presence of Goethe, and lived so
> much in his works, that any sensation or idea that came to him
> prompted him to ask himself: Would Goethe have felt or
> thought this way?

This dedication to the spirit of Goethe transmitted itself
from Schröer to his pupil. But it was in a different manner
that Goethe became Steiner's guiding star.

There was living in Vienna at the time a young authoress
named Marie Eugenie delle Grazie. When not yet sixteen she
had made an impression with an epic, *Herman*, a drama, *Saul*,
and a tale, *Die Zigeunerin* (The Gipsy Lass). The well-known
aesthete and philosopher Robert Zimmermann is believed to
have said of her that she was 'the only true genius that I have
ever met in my life'.

No sooner had Steiner read some of the poems of delle
Grazie than he wrote an article on them. This proved the
opportunity for a first meeting with her. She was living in the
house of the catholic priest and professor of Christian
philosophy Laurenz Müllner (1848–1911), who in 1894 was
Rector of the University of Vienna. He was the teacher of the
young poetess, who was alone in the world, and stood to her
in loco parentis. Together they formed one of the most active
centres of intellectual life in Vienna. Each week a circle of
leading personalities, artists, and scientists met there. The

atmosphere of these gatherings made a powerful appeal to the impressionable Steiner. It attracted and at the same time repelled him.

> The people who met there represented many different types of intellectual attainment. The poetess was the centre of attraction. She read her poems; she expressed her view of the world, driving her words home with emphatic gestures; she looked at human life in the light of her ideas. There was no sunlight. Always the dim light of the moon. Threatening clouds. From the habitations of men flames of fire shot upwards into the gloom, bearing with them as it were the passions and illusions by which men are devoured. But touching everything human, always arresting, the bitterness swept up in the spell cast by the noble charm of a personality that was spiritual through and through.

In the same period when Schröer, a protestant, was introducing him to the world of Goethe and thus laying the

Marie Eugenie delle Grazie (1864–1931)

foundations for his own 'Goetheanism', he encountered in Müllner a brand of cultivated catholicism which, consistent with its inner self, viewed Goethe with repugnance. The Müllner circle was powerfully attracted to the novels of Dostoyevsky with their masterly representations of human suffering. Shakespeare's dramas too, with their realistic portrayals of criminal humanity and the aberrations of fallible human nature, aroused avid interest in that circle. But delle Grazie and Müllner were united in their vehement dislike of Goethe.

> Delle Grazie exhibited something like a deep personal antipathy for Goethe. Delle Grazie's mansion was one in which pessimism and vitality were manifested together: the seat of Anti-Goetheanism.

It is typical of Rudolf Steiner's approach to life that he voluntarily exposed himself to the contrasting intellectual climates of Schröer and the delle Grazie circle. Schröer himself came only on the first evening. He did not come again. Steiner remained a regular guest for as long as he was able.

The rejection of Goethe by this circle did not disturb him. After all, it was one of his principles not to devote himself to a cause or a person until he had made himself familiar with it or its opposite. And thus in retrospect he was able to say that he was 'immeasurably indebted' to the circle around delle Grazie.

We here come face to face with a fundamental trait in Steiner's character, which was often to give rise to misunderstanding. This is his unusual interest in whatever was 'quite different' in the minds of his fellow human beings. Among his teachers and the friends of his youth Steiner found little true understanding of his own fundamental spiritual problems. He himself was very receptive to theirs.

The inevitable consequence was that his mind was as it were divided.

> My wrestling with the problems of cognition, with which I was at that time especially preoccupied, profoundly interested my friends but evoked little active sympathy. In my experience of these problems I was to a great extent alone. I on the other hand experienced to the full everything that occurred in the lives of my friends. Thus my life flowed in two streams; I followed one as a lonely wanderer, the other in the lively companionship of people whom I had learned to love.

This division between two existences, to both of which he was closely attached, gave Steiner pain. 'My emotional life was truly torn asunder, being divided between two sides, to both of which I was attached by true love and veneration.'

His relationship with his revered teacher is to be seen in the same light. Schröer had opened for him the way to Goethe.

> My mind responded with fullest sympathy to everything that came from Schröer. But even where he was concerned I could do no other than build up independently in my own mind the object of my spiritual striving. Schröer was an idealist, and the world of ideas was for him the driving force in natural and human creation. For me the idea was the shadow of a living spiritual world.

These are the words in his *Autobiography* with which Rudolf Steiner describes the gulf that separated him from Schröer, despite the close human relationship between them.

An outstanding figure in the circle of wits surrounding delle Grazie and Müllner was the priest of the Cistercian Order Wilhelm Neumann, renowned as scholar and churchman. Steiner enjoyed discussions with him, chiefly on the way home from the soirées.

Wilhelm Neumann (1837–1919)

I will mention only two of them here. One was about the essential being of Christ. I expressed my view that through supernatural influences Jesus of Nazareth had taken Christ into himself, and since the Mystery of Golgotha Christ has co-existed with the development of man as a spiritual essence. This conversation made a profound impression on my mind; it has emerged again and again, for it had profound significance for me. This was really a discussion between three: Professor Neumann, myself, and an invisible third person, the personification of Catholic Dogma, which accompanied Professor Neumann and appeared menacingly, visible to the spiritual eye, behind him, and tapped him reprovingly on the shoulder whenever the scholar's subtle logic brought him too close to agreement with me. It was remarkable how often with him the proposition was reversed by the conclusion. At that time I was face to face with the catholic church in the person of one of its worthiest representatives; through him I learned to respect it, but I also got to know it thoroughly.

On another occasion we talked about reincarnation. The Professor heard me out and named all kinds of literary works that had something to say about the subject; he frequently shook his head gently but obviously had no intention of going into the subject, which he appeared to find bizarre. And yet this conversation for me had significance. Neumann's discomposure at this confrontation between his unspoken opinions and my pronouncements is a lasting memory.

It is no mere chance that some forty years later Steiner recalled so exactly these two discussions with Wilhelm Neumann; for they were concerned with the two cardinal points of anthroposophy that Steiner was to develop later; christology and reincarnation.

On both these points Steiner not only found himself in a confrontation, through Neumann, with the dogmas of the church whose son he himself was but sensed the 'discomposure' that his ideas occasioned the representatives of Roman theology. He therefore could not but be aware that these discussions were a foretaste of much that he was to encounter in later life.

The Vienna coffee houses of that era have become world-famous. A large part of the intellectual life of the Austrian Empire went on in them. Political decisions were taken in them, poems and novels were written, and above all, one knew whom one would meet in them, at what time, and in what places.

'I often recall the discussions, some of them interminable, that took place in a well-known coffee house on the Michaeler Platz in Vienna.'

Steiner is referring here to the 'Griensteidl' Café. For a time he used it as a postal address, since though all else were in doubt he would assuredly turn up at 'Griensteidl'.

Many of those with whom Steiner associated in Vienna and who were household names even outside Vienna are today

forgotten. Names like those of the poet Fercher von Stein-
wand and the composer Stross will hardly be remembered
today.

Another personality who had a major influence on Steiner
in Vienna was Rosa Mayreder. He met her in the house of
Marie Lang, the theosophist. This was a woman entirely
different in nature from Eugenie delle Grazie, but for Steiner
no less significant. They soon became close friends.

> Rosa Mayreder was one of the persons whom I have met in my
> life for whom I have had the greatest admiration. I followed
> her career with the greatest interest. This woman appeared to
> me to possess all the intellectual gifts that are humanly
> attainable in such a degree that their harmonious working
> made of her the epitome of everything that is human.

Rosa Mayreder was a painter, authoress, and poetess. She

S. Griensteidl's Coffee House in Vienna
(on Michaeler Platz, at the corner of Herrengasse)

*Rosa Mayreder
(1858–1938)*

was known at the time for her two-volume work 'Critique of Womanliness'. She wrote the libretto for Hugo Wolf's opera *Corregidor*. Later, jointly with Marie Lang, she edited the woman's magazine *Dokumente der Frauen*. She was a warm-hearted protagonist of that struggle for women's liberation that is hardly talked about today, and that yet cleared the way for the equality of the sexes.

The pessimism that was the keynote of delle Grazie's temperament was alien to Rosa Mayreder. She was an extrovert with a powerful, positive creative urge—though anything but the typical 'suffragette'. She was a woman of her time and confidently tackled the task that fell to her. In her struggle for freedom she found in Rudolf Steiner a kindred soul.

During these years Rudolf Steiner was mentally shaping his thoughts on his personal theory of knowledge, which later was to bear fruit in his book *Philosophy of Freedom*.

Rosa Mayreder was the person with whom, more than with anyone else, I discussed these outlines at the time that my book was taking shape. She partly broke down the inner isolation in which I have lived ... And in later life I have often gratefully called to mind some memory—the memory for instance of a walk through the glorious alpine forests during which Rosa Mayreder and I discussed the true meaning of human freedom.

This friendship outlasted the Vienna period. There are many letters to prove this. A year after Rudolf Steiner had moved to Weimar, Rosa Mayreder wrote to him: 'I am daily, hourly conscious of the void left in my life since your departure, whenever, in countless moments of reflection when uncertainty, doubt, confusion, anxiety, evoke the desire for the lost happiness of those friendly discussions with you. The longer you are away, dear friend, the more intolerable I find it that you should remain away.' (Vienna, 26 October 1890.)

Steiner as a Private Tutor

Rudolf Steiner's early life contained the presage of something that was to bear fruit in the last year of his life: therapeutic education. On the recommendation of Professor Karl Julius Schröer, in 1884 he became private tutor in the family of Ladislaus and Pauline Specht, remaining there until he left Vienna in 1890.

A special task fell to my lot in the field of education. I was recommended as tutor to a family in which there were four boys. As far as concerned three of them, my task was merely to give them the preliminary instruction for entry into the elementary school, and after that to coach them for the middle school. The fourth, who was about ten years old, was at first handed over to me entirely to educate. He was his parents' problem child, particularly his mother's. When I first arrived, he had hardly mastered the very first rudiments of reading, writing, and arithmetic. He was considered to be physically and mentally abnormal to such an extent as to lead the family to doubt whether he was possible to educate at all. His thought processes were slow and sluggish. Even slight mental exertion brought on headaches, loss of vitality, pallor, and disturbing mental symptoms. . . .

I had the satisfaction of seeing the boy in two years make up the deficiencies in his elementary school studies and pass the grammar school entrance examination. His health too had improved considerably. The hydrocephaly from which he had suffered was regressing rapidly. I felt justified in recommending his parents to send him to an ordinary school.

I thank the good fortune that brought me this personal relationship. For through it I gained firsthand knowledge of what constitutes the essence of humanity, such as I do not

Rudolf Steiner as a student.
Vienna, about 1882

believe I could have gained in so tangible a form in any other way....

My charge was able to pass through grammar school. I remained at his side until he reached the lower sixth. He had by then advanced so far that he no longer needed my help. After passing out of grammar school he entered medical school and fell in the World War in the exercise of his calling....

A large part of my youth was bound up with the task which fell to me in this way.

Rudolf Steiner later recalled with profound gratitude the time when he lived with the Specht family and the duty that was assigned to him of caring for the boy—his name was Otto Specht—and putting him on the road to health. It was indeed a kindly fate that imposed on him so early in life the duty of devoting himself to the real problems of health and sickness. Without this six years' apprenticeship he could hardly have been in a position later to become the inaugurator of a movement for therapeutic education.

RUDOLF STEINER THE GOETHE SCHOLAR

Karl Julius Schröer had recommended Rudolf Steiner to Joseph Kürschner, who was then working in association with a staff of scholars on an edition of Goethe's works in his Deutsche National-Litteratur series. The intention was that Steiner should edit Goethe's scientific works. At twenty-one, he was by far the youngest of this band of commentators. The first volume appeared in 1884. Schröer wrote the preface. When a modern reader opens this, the first of Steiner's major works, the description that forces itself upon him is 'budding genius'. It is beyond comprehension how a man of such tender years, who through study at the polytechnic had acquired the bare rudiments of modern science, could prove

Joseph Kürschner
(1855–1902)

equal to the task assigned him. Right up to the present day no better, that is to say more appreciative, commentary has been written on Goethe's botanical and zoological writings. It is irrelevant to point to any minor errors that Steiner may have been guilty of. The key to the whole is the unique situation in which Goethe found himself in his quest over many decades for a new and different understanding of the organic sciences. It wounded Goethe deeply not to be taken up on what to him was a weighty matter. 'It is the greatest torment not to be understood.' (*Schicksal der Druckschrift*)

Goethe published his 'Metamorphosis of the Plant', which with its introductions may assuredly be looked on as the programme for a new science of organic nature, without defining exactly the particular position that it was to occupy in the history of science. This was not his way. He was more likely to refer to fundamental principles in a fundamental note. Thus, in the introduction: 'We need only remind the

Friedrich Theodor Vischer (1807–1887)

friends of science in a few words of what chemistry and anatomy have contributed to our insight into and general understanding of nature. But these persistent efforts to break everything down into its parts entail many disadvantages. For while life can be broken into its elements, it cannot be reconstructed out of them and revitalized.' Goethe believed that he had found an alternative method to replace the 'dismemberment' of life. He attempted to lay the foundations of this new method that was to put the organic world in its true perspective.

Steiner rediscovered for his generation this 'forgotten Goethe':

'Goethe is the Copernicus and the Kepler of the organic world.'

This is what Rudolf Steiner wrote in his introduction, and he devoted almost fifteen years to proving the truth of this proposition, which the nineteenth century had been unable to accept. Before further volumes of Kürschner's Deutsche National-Litteratur appeared (1887, 1890, and following), Steiner had published his own thoughts on the new organic science in his book: *A Theory of Knowledge.*

In this early work he does something that Goethe had always avoided—he reflected on his own thinking. But this had to be done if he was to prove that Goethe's method of studying nature was 'scientific'.

From Brunn am Gebirge, to which place his father's work had caused his parents to move, he sent to the then well-known aesthete and author Friedrich Theodor Vischer (1807–1887) in reference to letters he had exchanged with him four years previously, a copy of this work accompanied by a highly informative letter: 'If it'—his own theory of knowledge—

also has a bearing on Goethe, I freely confess that my purpose has been to make a contribution to the theory of knowledge, not to the study of Goethe. For what concerns me in Goethe's world philosophy is, not his positive pronouncements but the general drift of his thoughts on the world. For me, Goethe's and Schiller's statements about science form a centre whose beginning and end must be sought. The beginning: by exhibiting principles which we have to conceive of as supporting this world view; the end: by analyzing the consequences of this way of looking at things for our own view of the world and life.

Vischer took this letter seriously enough that it was found among his literary remains. Unfortunately his reply has never been found. The work itself is a clear exposition of the standpoint he had adopted in his letter to Vischer. The old vitalistic and teleological theories of the eighteenth and the first half of the nineteenth century were of little service in founding a valid science of botany, because of their purely speculative character, but the physical-mechanistic methods developed later are equally ineffectual.

People have the idea that they have to think about objects in a certain way, and indeed about *every* object—about the whole universe—in the same way.

The method of physics is simply a *special* case of a general method of scientific research which takes into account the nature of the objects under study as far as concerns their relation to the field covered by the science. Extend the application of this method to the organic field and you override its essential nature. Instead of studying the organic world in the way that its essential nature requires, you force it to accept an alien set of laws. And so by denying to the organic world its essential nature you fail to recognize it for what it is. This type of scientific procedure simply repeats at a higher level the methods that have proved successful at a lower level.

To the extent that inorganic processes also take place in organisms, there is justification for applying the physical-chemical method to biology. But when what it is all about is

From a notebook of Rudolf Steiner's about 1890: 'Goethe studied
the subjective colours by tracing them back to fundamental phenomena, not by seeking the causes in the anatomy of the organs. He
looks for the conditions in which distinct phenomena occur. He does
not kill the organism but studies life, even here'.

what makes a plant a plant, an animal an animal, the mechanistic method is of no avail. A rose, an ear of corn, a deer, a lion, have never been derived from the periodical system of chemical elements, and never will be. The objectives as such of biology lie in a field in which it is meaningless to apply the concept 'chemical element'. The concepts to which Goethe sought to give clear definition and which he worked out in painstaking detail, such as archetypal plant, (Ger. *Urpflanze*), type, polarity, and intensification, will lead somewhere if biologists apply them with the same care that 'exact' physicists and chemists usually employ.

For Steiner, it was not a *return* to Goethe, nor to the Goetheanists. All honour to the achievements of Carus, Oken, Batsch, Alexander Braun, to name only a few, but they were unable to bring to a halt the triumphal march of the mechanists and materialists in the second half of the nineteenth century and the first half of the twentieth.

Even the more or less ineffectual experiments of the 'totality' theorists such as Driesch and holists like Smuts were unable to put up an effective opposition to the 'mechanists'. They all lacked the fundamental asset of a theory of knowledge which would have given them the same right as the physicists and chemists to work at biology, psychology, and pneumatology. What Rudolf Steiner was seeking in the years from 1882 to 1896 was just such a philosophical basis for a science of the organic that was to overcome materialism.

Weimar

Karl Julius Schröer brought Steiner to the notice of the management committee of the Goethe-and-Schiller Archives at Weimar, and he was invited to go to Weimar. In August 1889 he paid his first visit there. Bernhard Suphan, the Director of the Archives, settled with him the details of their

Work programme agreed between Suphan and Rudolf Steiner

future collaboration there. He was to edit the scientific writings as his share of the work on the great Sophien-Ausgabe.

Steiner was in a state of pleasurable excitement. On 9 August he wrote to Richard Specht:

The Goethe-and-Schiller Archives at Weimar

There is a quite special feeling about knowing that one has beneath one's feet the ground that the German masters trod. I do not mean Weimar alone. For I must tell you I have known few days in my life comparable to yesterday, when I entered Luther's room in the Wartburg.... There can be few places in Germany that affect us as does the Wartburg, with which so many historical memories are associated. It is a pity that I can only see it all *en passant*, what with all the work I have to do at the Archives. I have learned a great deal here, a very great deal. I find it very difficult to tear myself away from these treasures. I live just behind the Goethehaus, and on my way to the Archives every morning I pass by the house of Frau von Stein. All these things are very precious to me.

Standing for the first time before the splendid statue, I felt as though new life was infused into all my meditations and thoughts about Schiller and Goethe, as though a special kind of life-bringing air was being wafted over everything.

On the way back from Weimar, Steiner made a detour via Berlin to visit Eduard von Hartmann. A lively discussion ensued between them. A year later, in the autumn of 1890, he took his final departure from Vienna and made the move to Weimar.

The commencement of Steiner's work at the Goethe-and-Schiller Archives at Weimar, which was under the patronage of the Grand Duchess Sophie, is recorded in the 12th volume of the *Goethe-Jahrbuch* (Goethe Almanac): 'From the autumn of 1890, the regular workers were joined by Rudolf Steiner from Vienna. The entire file of morphology (except for osteology) was entrusted to him, five or possibly six volumes in the second section. In the manuscript remains

Bernard Suphan, Director of the Goethe-and-Schiller Archives, in his study, 1909

there is some highly important material that belongs in these volumes.'

Rudolf Steiner performed his task conscientiously—but never with an eye to philology alone. He was generally recognized as the leading expert on Goethe's scientific writings. Doubts were sometimes cast on his philological accuracy. Candidly he admitted: 'This person'—he means himself—'has never taken pride in philological activity as such, he could indeed himself point to many errors in this regard and does not wish to extenuate his many solecisms.'

In Vienna, Rudolf Steiner had felt at home. Not only was he by birth an Austrian. He had a fair measure of the simple cordiality and good will so typical of Vienna. And throughout his life his speech retained its Austrian flavour. In Weimar he was, and remained, a guest. As a guest, he approached with deepest reverence, and at first with the highest hopes, the German Athens, that had once—if only for a short while—

Rudolf Steiner at Weimar, 1889

The University of Rostock

been the centre of the world's intellectual history. But Rudolf Steiner soon began to feel profoundly disappointed. Not so much in what he saw of the social life of Weimar. Of course, as far as social life was concerned Vienna had spoilt him. But in Weimar there were circles of authors, scholars, and artists, where Rudolf Steiner, who thought of himself as a 'sociable person', felt at ease and was accepted. But the kind of pedantic philology that was practised at the Goethe-and-Schiller Archives, his actual place of work at Weimar, chilled him and drove him into isolation. Thus, on 20 October 1890 he wrote to Rosa Mayreder: 'Here I am all alone. There is no one here who has the remotest understanding of what motivates me and what goes on in my mind.' And he wrote in the same mood to one of his Vienna friends (Friedrich Eckstein) in November 1890: 'You can have little idea how alone I feel here, and how little understood.' He had come to Weimar full of the greatest expectations, as though on a pilgrimage to a holy land. Now he complains: 'Here in Weimar, the home of the classical mummies, I stand coldly aside from the life and activity (May 1891).'

Steiner was dogged by this feeling of spiritual isolation throughout the Weimar years, despite frequent meetings with important, and in their day, distinguished persons like Treitschke, Herman Grimm, Ernst Haeckel, Gabriele Reuter, Fritz Koegel, and many more.

He bore his exile for almost seven years. Nor did he merely bear with it. At this period of his life, in addition to doing his work on the Sophien-Ausgabe he laid the philosophical foundation for the science of the spirit which he called 'Anthroposophy'.

Next from Weimar, he proceeded to his long overdue graduation as Doctor of Philosophy at Rostock. The Rostock philosopher Heinrich von Stein had aroused Rudolf Steiner's interest through his work *Sieben Bücher Platonismus*. 'It was because of this that I submitted my dissertation to him. I

*Eduard von Hartmann
(1843–1906)*

Heinrich von Stein (1833–1896), who accepted Rudolf Steiner's PhD thesis at Rostock University

esteemed the good old philosopher on account of his book, but I met him only at the examination.' At this one meeting, Heinrich von Stein impressed his personality on Steiner:

> His entire deportment bespoke calm. He was elderly, with a mild eye, as if for directing with gentle insistence the development of his students; in every sentence that he spoke the words bore the accent of philosophic reflection ... He said to me: 'Your dissertation is not the sort of thing that is required; it is evident that it was not prepared under the guidance of a professor; but its content is such that I shall be happy to accept it.'

The title of the dissertation translates as: 'The fundamental problem of the theory of knowledge, with particular reference to Fichte's philosophy. Prolegomena to the reconciliation of the philosophical consciousness with itself.'

Steiner's central problem could not have been more clearly

formulated: prolegomena to the reconciliation of the philosophical consciousness with itself. This was the very thing
that Goethe had never attempted. His contemplation of
nature was a spontaneous outgrowth of his own essential
being. One is tempted to coin the paradoxical phrase 'instinct
of the intellect' to describe Goethe's posture. Thus for all that
Goethe's work contained as portents of the future, Goethe
was for Steiner an end to which, by 'reflecting on thinking',
by the 'reconciliation of the intellectual consciousness with
itself', he proposed to make a new beginning, and really did
so. The gist of his dissertation appeared one year later under
the title: *Truth and science. Prologue to a 'philosophy of
freedom'. Dedicated with deepest respect to Dr Eduard von
Hartmann 1892.*

Gabriele Reuter

In Weimar, at the house of the author Olden, whose sociable
circle he often frequented, Rudolf Steiner made the
acquaintance of Gabriele Reuter. She was at that time
working on her novel *Aus guter Familie* (Well-connected),
which was to make her widely known. 'There was something
ineffably beautiful about the admiration of the Olden circle
for Gabriele Reuter.' And Steiner shared whole-heartedly in
the admiration for this remarkable woman.

> Some of the most glorious hours of my life were spent in the
> company of Gabriele Reuter.... Her personality was beset by
> deep human problems, with which she grappled with a certain
> radicalism of the heart and the emotions. She accepted whole-
> heartedly the challenge of every situation in social life where
> traditional prejudice appeared to conflict with the primal
> demands of human nature.

Looking back on the struggle for emancipation and the
striving to give women a dignified role in society, which was

Gabriele Reuter
(1859–1941)

conducted with such utter commitment in the last two decades of the last century, we are entitled to say that Gabriele
Reuter was one of the noblest champions of this struggle for
liberation. She is today almost forgotten. In his *Autobiography* Steiner rescues her from oblivion and speaks of his
gratitude to her:

> There was an infinite charm about the conversations that one
> had with her. Looking back, I can recall standing with her at a
> street corner in blazing sunshine for more than an hour dis-
> cussing the questions that moved her. Gabriele Reuter could
> talk with the utmost dignity and without for a moment losing
> her composure of things the mention of which would imme-
> diately throw others into a state of visible excitement. What-
> ever she had to say, Gabriele Reuter spoke with pronounced
> emphasis; but she conveyed this emphasis, not vocally, but
> entirely mentally. I believe that this gift of speaking at a
> constant pitch and articulating entirely at the mental level was

peculiar to her. And it seems to me that in her writing this idiosyncrasy has been developed all round until it became her enchanting style.

Anna Eunike

In Weimar Steiner experienced the vexations of the hunt for accommodation, but this ended when he found a home with a family that sheltered him and saw to all his needs. Captain Eugen Friedrich Eunike, retired, had died in 1882. He left a wife, Anna Eunike, née Schultz, and five children, four girls and a boy. Rudolf Steiner became part of this family and lived with them for the greater part of the Weimar period.

> Part of the house was allotted to me; Frau Anna Eunike, who soon became my close friend, saw to all my needs in the most selfless way. She was very anxious for my assistance in the difficult task of educating her children.... I only saw the

Anna Steiner, née Schultz, former married name Eunike (1853–1911)

children when the opportunity was created. This often happened, for I was treated as just one of the family. But except in the morning and evening I had my meals elsewhere. In the congenial family circle in which I found myself I felt really at ease, but that was not all; for when the younger members of the visiting Goethegesellschaft from Berlin, who had attached themselves closely to me, wanted to get together in congenial surroundings, they used to visit me at the Eunike house. And I have every reason to think that they enjoyed themselves there.

Among the frequenters of these social evenings was Otto Erich Hartleben, who was to be closely associated with Rudolf Steiner in the first Berlin period.

Haeckel and Nietzsche

At the time when Steiner came to Weimar the controversy about Darwinism, in which Ernst Haeckel was conducting

Friedrich Nietzsche (1844–1900)

from Jena the argument in favour of materialistic monism, was reaching its climax. At this time Friedrich Nietzsche, sick, and inaccessible to almost all visitors, was living in isolation in Naumburg. During and after the Weimar period, Rudolf Steiner's fate was to involve him with Haeckel and Nietzsche in the most singular manner.

As different as Haeckel from Nietzsche were the encounters that Steiner had with the two of them.

In Vienna in 1889 he had for the first time read some of Nietzsche's works. The Nietzsche phenomenon had a fascination for him. Nietzsche seemed to him a highly significant intellectual phenomenon, one that was to be taken seriously. It was not in Steiner's nature to become an 'adherent' of Haeckel or Nietzsche. But he did not join in the opposition to them, which came above all from the church, and was always to be found on their side. In 1895 Steiner became active in the controversy about Nietzsche with the publication of his book: *Friedrich Nietzsche, Fighter for Freedom.*

Shortly before I was preparing for the writing of this book, Nietzsche's sister, Elisabeth Förster-Nietzsche, presented herself at the Goethe-and-Schiller Archives. She was preparing for the setting up of the Nietzsche archives and wanted to find out how the Goethe-and-Schiller Archives were organized. Shortly afterwards the publisher of Nietzsche's works, Fritz Koegel, turned up in Weimar, and I got to know him.

Later I was to clash violently with Elisabeth Förster-Nietzsche. At that time her lively, engaging mind appealed to me greatly.

These clashes caused me the deepest pain; they were brought about by a highly complex situation; I was under the necessity of defending myself against accusations; I know that all this was necessary; I also know that the many happy hours that I spent at the Nietzsche archives at Naumburg and Weimar are now remembered with a touch of bitterness.

... But I am still grateful to Frau Förster-Nietzsche for taking me into Friedrich Nietzsche's room on the occasion of the first of the many visits that I paid her. There he lay in mental darkness on a sofa. I was struck by the nobility of his brow—the brow of an artist and thinker. It was early afternoon: Those eyes in which, though the fire in them was dead the workings of the soul could still be read, took in his surroundings but conveyed no image to his mind. One just stood there, and to Nietzsche it meant nothing. But looking at that face that was so eloquent of the spirit it was almost possible to believe that this was the expression of a soul which had spent the morning piecing together thoughts and now desired to rest awhile. My soul was seized by an inner convulsion, which could have been interpreted as understanding of the genius whose gaze was directed towards me but did not meet my eyes. The passivity of that prolonged stare blocked the understanding in my own gaze, so that I saw but encountered no response.

I could think only haltingly about what I had seen; and these halting thoughts are the content of my book, *Nietzsche, a Man against his Time*. But the halting nature of this book cannot obscure the fact that it was Nietzsche who inspired it.

Other articles on Nietzsche followed the publication of this book. Such for instance are: 'The Philosophy of Friedrich Nietzsche as a Pyscho-pathological Problem' and 'The Personality of Friedrich Nietzsche and Psychopathology'. Both were published in the *Wiener Klinische Rundschau*.

After Nietzsche's death Steiner on a number of occasions made speeches in commemoration of him—for instance, to the circle of 'Die Kommenden' (The Coming Generation) on 13 September 1900, in Berlin.

Nietzsche foundered on his own failure to strike the spark of true spirit out of the scientific age. Rudolf Steiner watched with the deepest sympathy and interest Nietzsche's anguished, earnest striving and his downfall, but continued on his way undeterred.

Steiner's enthusiastic approval of Ernst Haeckel was a stumbling block to many. Was not the philosophy of the 'Pope of Monism', as his opponents loved to call Haeckel, incompatible with the Goethean thinking which Steiner had advocated from 1882 onwards and which underlay the concepts which were later to lead him to formulate his 'Anthroposophy'? How was it possible for the same man who had expressed the quintessence of his theory of knowledge in the sentence: 'Awakening to the idea in reality is the true communion of humanity', to dedicate his work on 'Thoughts on the World and on Life in the 19th Century' to the author of a work such as *Riddle of the Universe* '1899' which was the classical exposition of plain, unvarnished materialism? How could a man of independent mind, with cogent ideas of his own, speak out, write a Philosophy of Freedom, and at the same time approve a work that states with conviction 'There is no God, no immortality, and no freedom of the human soul'?

Ernst Haeckel (1834–1910)

One thing is certain; Rudolf Steiner was not among the countless opponents of Haeckel. It appeared to him that at the transition from the nineteenth to the twentieth century what Haeckel had to say was of greater moment than anything that the Christian theologians could advance against them and in defence of their own position. Rudolf Steiner was convinced that the theory of evolution, of which Darwin and Haeckel were the pioneers, simply must be absorbed in the modern consciousness. Even though the first attempts to portray the origins, in particular the assertions made about the effective causes of evolution, were primitive and rough-hewn—Rudolf Steiner accepted the fundamental notion of the evolution of life. He could not but see it as a weak point in the theologian's case that they suppressed the facts of nature and stood helpless when confronted with the findings of science about the evolution of nature and man.

> Far more dangerous than the damage done by the belief of immature minds in our descent from the apes is the campaign that, with the approval of theologians and other reactionaries, has been conducted for decades past against the theory of origins.

Ernst Haeckel battled with enthusiasm against an outdated world philosophy in the naive belief that the new science of nature and its evolution would point the way forward to a valid world philosophy. But he was unable to perceive how inadequately he was equipped for expressing his thoughts on the subject which he had at heart.

> If Haeckel had studied even just a little philosophy, in which he was not merely a dilettante, but a child, he would assuredly have drawn from his epoch-making phylogenetic studies the loftiest spiritualistic conclusions.
>
> Now, despite German philosophy, despite all else in German education, Haeckel's thinking on phylogenetics is the

most significant fact of German intellectual life in the second half of the nineteenth century. And there is no better foundation for occultism than Haeckel's theory. Haeckel's theory is great, and Haeckel the poorest commentator on it. We do the best service to culture, not by exhibiting Haeckel's shortcomings to our contemporaries but by demonstrating to them the greatness of his phylogenetic thinking. This is what I have done in the two volumes of my *Thoughts on the World and on Life in the 19th Century*, which in fact I dedicated to Haeckel, and in my small work *Haeckel and his Opponents*.

For a number of years Steiner and Haeckel communicated with each other only by letters. 'In the first instance I had no need to become personally acquainted with Haeckel, although I had occasion to think about him a great deal.'

On the occasion of his 60th birthday in 1894 Haeckel was honoured at Jena with magnificent festivities, and Steiner was one of those who received an invitation. At Steiner's request, Haeckel's son introduced him to his father at the banquet:

That was how I made the personal acquaintance of Haeckel. He was an enchanting person. He looked out on the world with eyes that held an expression that was so naive, so mild, that one felt it must dissolve under the impact of thought. He could bear sense impressions only, not the thoughts that manifest themselves in objects and processes. Haeckel's every motion was directed towards giving due emphasis to what the senses express, and not to revealing the thoughts which govern the motion. I realized why it was that Haeckel so enjoyed painting. He spent himself in the contemplation of the senses. At the point where thinking begins his mind ceased its activity and sought rather to retain what it had seen through the medium of the paint brush. This was the essential nature of Haeckel. Had he given it rein, something of an unusual charm and humanity would have been seen.

But in one corner of his soul something was stirring, something that was obstinately trying to express itself as thought, something that came from a quite different quarter than his feeling for nature...

...There were two contrasting elements in Haeckel. He was a man who had *a gentle, love-inspired feeling for nature*, but in the background was a kind of phantom with inchoate thoughts and stunted ideas which breathed *fanaticism*. When Haeckel spoke, his mildness was such that it was hard for his fanaticism to find expression in words; it was as though his innate gentleness interposed to tone down the effect of the daemonic utterances. A human enigma whom seeing one could not but love; whose judgments often enraged one. This was Haeckel as I saw him in the nineties of the last century when he was preparing what was to lead to the violent controversy that raged around his ideas at the turn of the century.

The subject of Haeckel cropped up again and again throughout Steiner's life, right up to the end. In no fewer than 25 publications and innumerable lectures the name of Haeckel occurs.

STRIVING FOR PERCEPTION IN THE
WEIMAR PERIOD

In the Weimar period, Steiner's spiritual and intellectual situation was an unusual one; but equally unusual was the strength of the conviction which enabled him to master it.

> I was then at an age when the mind follows its bent and turns the full weight of its attention on the external world, seeking to forge links with it. For me, the philosophical ideas that were current—those of Nietzsche and Haeckel, for instance—were part of the external world. And I was made aware how little, basically, I had lived in the external world. Whenever I withdrew from active pursuits it was borne in upon me that up to that time the only world that was familiar to me had been the spiritual world that I contemplated within myself. With this world I found it easy to communicate. And I often thought to myself how difficult it had been for me throughout my childhood and youth to communicate with the external world through the senses. I have always had difficulty in committing to memory the data which it is essential to have at one's finger tips, for instance in the field of science. I had to see natural objects repeatedly before I could remember what they are called, what is their scientific classification etc. Indeed I may say that the world of the senses was a world of shadows and images. It passed before my mind in images, whereas my communion with the spiritual world had all the true semblance of reality.

It would be tempting on the strength of this description of himself to label Steiner 'introvert'. But in his case this diagnosis would be wide of the mark.

It is true that he added: 'I remained shut up within myself. It was as if a thin wall separated me from the external world.' But the really distinctive feature of Steiner's internal situation at the age of about thirty-five was the constant breaching of this outer wall—not without attendant suffering—and the crossing over to the world of thought and sensation of the 'quite-other', almost to the point of self-surrender.

> In my own mind I lived in a world which bordered on the external world; but I always needed to cross a frontier when I wanted to have any communication with the external world; I led an active life; but in every single instance I had to pass out of my world so to speak through a door in order to get into the stream of this activity. So that whenever I approached the external world I felt as if I was paying a visit. But this did not stop me from taking a very active part in whatever was going on at the place I was visiting. And during my visit I felt quite at home.

This account by Steiner of his own situation is the key to the extreme difficulties experienced by not entirely well-

Rudolf Steiner in Weimar, 1896

disposed biographers. When he was writing about Darwin
and Haeckel, then to a not too careful observer it might
appear that he was an adherent of Darwinism. If he took up
the cudgels on behalf of Nietzsche he was taken for a follower
of Nietzsche. And so on.

> Thus it was with people, thus with philosophies. I enjoyed a
> visit to Suphan, I enjoyed a visit to Hartleben. Suphan never
> visited Hartleben; Hartleben never visited Suphan. Neither
> could enter into the other's way of thinking and feeling. I felt
> *as if* at home with both Suphan and Hartleben. But neither
> Suphan nor Hartleben actually came to me. Even if they
> visited me they remained within themselves.

It was not he, but the *others*, who were introverted. Steiner
is not alone in maintaining this. Men whom he met in his life
have borne witness to it, among them Edouard Schuré, Jules
Sauerwein, Christian Morgenstern, Friedrich Rittelmeyer,
Albert Steffen. They, and many others, have noted the
extraordinary gift that Steiner possessed of being able so to
speak to slip into his antagonist's skin and in so doing often to
understand him, and even interpret him, better than he could
himself.

This was how he stood in relation to the ideologies of
Haeckel and Nietzsche.

> I felt that relatively speaking they were justified. My mental
> make-up was such that I could not say of them: that is right,
> that is wrong. Had I done so I should have been bound to feel
> that what was alive in them was alien to me. But I felt neither
> to be more alien than the other; for I felt at home only in the
> spiritual world that I contemplated, while I could feel 'as if at
> home' in any other world.

Because he dwelt so secure in his own spiritual world there
was no risk of his succumbing to a kind of relativism deprived
of all character and of understanding everything without

maintaining a position of his own. One of the principles of the anthroposophy that he worked out at a later date was the relative justification of a number of different ideologies. According to Steiner there is the truth of idealism, of materialism, of empiricism, and so on, just as there is the truth according to Fichte, Herbart, Marx, etc. His aim was an all-embracing view which allows for various slants and intellectual standpoints—and yet avoids syncretism.

> He who rejects everything that is not in line with his thinking will not be upset by the notion that the various ideologies can, relatively speaking, be justified. He can experience without mental reservation the fascination of thoughts which have been developed in a certain direction. So many people know what it is to be fascinated by intellectual activity. They make light of everything that does not fall in with their way of thinking. But whoever has his own world of contemplation, such as the spiritual world can only be, is aware of the justification for the different 'standpoints'; and he must be on his guard and not lean more towards the one than towards the other.
>
> This was the way I lived, not without spiritual dangers and difficulties.

In the seven years or so that he spent at Weimar, Rudolf Steiner published 95 titles. In addition to the seven volumes of the Sophien-Ausgabe, the remaining volumes in Kürschner's National-Litteratur, his dissertation, which he revised and to which he gave the title *Truth and Science*, and his book on Nietzsche, Steiner wrote his standard work of philosophy: *The Philosophy of Freedom*.

THE PHILOSOPHY OF FREEDOM

Awakening to the idea in reality is the true communion of
humanity.

Rudolf Steiner, 1887

The Philosophy of Freedom embodies, purely in the form of
thought, essentially everything that was to be the content of
the anthroposophy that Steiner developed later. It therefore
goes far beyond the scope of a monograph to describe the
contents of this book. Nevertheless we shall attempt to
sketch the outlines of this standard work of Steiner on the
theory of knowledge, written in his middle years. *The
Philosophy of Freedom* is sub-titled: 'The result of observing
the human soul as natural science observes nature'. This sub–
title clearly shows what was Steiner's concern. His aim is to
develop a science of the mind by the rigorous method of
natural science, but his search embraces both the natural and
the supernatural world. The natural world, that part of the
world that is accessible to study only through the senses and
their extensions, the microscope, the telescope, and so on,
remains *maya*, remains illusion, unless it is permeated by
conscious thought. The natural world is never the whole
truth. Only active thought that is not enslaved to sense-per-
ception but operates on the spiritual plane without being
shackled to the senses is able by the act of cognition to raise
the half-reality of the natural world to the fullness of reality.
By the exercise of this power of thought without sense-
perception man oversteps in spirit the frontiers which in
nineteenth century thinking on the theory of knowledge from
the time of Kant onwards had been held to be fixed for all
time and unassailable. It was above all this dogma of the

essential limitation of human knowledge that Steiner was out to challenge. In his own experience as a thinker Steiner had known what it was to cross that frontier that the intellect marks out for itself by limiting itself of its own accord to the study of those things only that have 'dimension, number, and weight'. In non-sensual thought, the mind is active on the spiritual plane. Seen as an activity of the spirit, thinking that is independent of the senses is linked to the spiritual world. The more intensively—creatively—spiritually the power of non-sensual thinking is deployed, the more conscious is it that it is rooted in the first cause of existence. Therefore:

> Talk of the limits of knowledge was meaningless to me. To me, knowing was the rediscovery of the spiritual substance of whatever was experienced by the soul in the perceived world. When people spoke of the limits of knowledge, I saw this as an admission that they were unable to experience true reality in themselves and hence were unable to recognize it in the real world. In putting forward my own views I was primarily concerned to refute the notion that there are limits of knowledge.

It is obvious that at any given time there are limits to the cognition of an individual. The limits of cognition of a child are progressively extended as the personality achieves maturity. They are not set once and for all but keep pace with human development. But this development takes place in two fields: that of perception and that of thought. Knowledge comes from the permeation of what is perceived by thought which has the power to create concepts.

> It is not the fault of objects, but of our own intellectual organization, that they first present themselves to us without the accompanying concepts. The way we function as beings, the elements that constitute reality reach us in two ways: through cognition and through thought.

By perception, Steiner does not merely mean sense–perception. The mental experience of feeling comes under the heading of perception. Feelings are organs of perception, in the same way as the eyes and the ears. The seeker after knowledge is required to look at what he has subjectively observed in the same objective way as he does at the information furnished by the scientific apparatus that he uses in his experiments. Therefore, from one aspect progress in knowledge is essentially linked to the training, refinement, and extension of the powers of observation. But the observation of the world at every level of physical, mental, and spiritual life is still not knowledge. Knowledge comes only with the intervention of thought purged of all non-spiritual elements. What are we to understand by purified thought? The purging of all irrelevant factors, such as wishes, inclinations, emotions, affects, illusions of all kinds! All the more need for a student of the supernatural to be governed by the same objectivity in this quest for knowledge as is required in scientific experiments.

> Observation is thus neither final nor conclusive, it is only one aspect of total reality. The other aspect is the concept. Cognition is the synthesis of observation and concept. Only the observation and conception of an object can make it complete.

The synthesis of observation and concept does not come about of itself, it is the result of the mental activity of the thinker. Only if the thought process is not disturbed by wishes, instincts, impulses, passions can it be said to be free. If a person acts under impulses which he uncritically allows to influence the thought processes that determine his actions, he is not free. It is not he, but the *it* of the emotions that govern him, that acts.

> He allows the non-spiritual part of him freedom of action. The spiritual part of him acts only if the impulses behind his acts

are derived as moral intuition from his non-sensual thinking. Then he, and no one else, acts. He is then a being who acts freely, in character with himself.

We thus see that for Steiner the problem of crossing the frontiers of knowledge is closely bound up with the problem of human freedom.

My purpose was to show that a man who will not accept that non-sensual thinking is a purely spiritual element in mankind will never be able to comprehend freedom; whereas when the reality of non-sensual thinking dawns on a man, comprehension comes.

To this extent the degree of freedom attained by someone is determined by the quality of his thinking. He who is unable to experience what Steiner calls non-sensual thinking as an activity inside himself, or is unable to imagine to himself such internal activity triggered off by non-sensual thinking, will not be able to follow Steiner or understand his philosophy of freedom. In speaking of non-sensual thinking Steiner is as it were drawing on his own experience. By this kind of thinking man ascends to the plane of the ethical ideal. Here thoughts and ideas are to him concrete objects, just like tables and chairs on the physical plane. Man is spiritually active when he is an observer on the spiritual plane and by virtue of this capability uses his moral imagination to make his own personal choices.

To be free means to possess the power to apply one's moral imagination to defining the conceptions (motives) that determine one's actions. Freedom is impossible if something outside myself (a mechanical process or an inferred god who is outside the world) determines my moral conceptions. I am free only to the extent that I produce these conceptions myself; I am not free if the reasons for my actions have been implanted in me by another being. A free being is one who can *will* what he himself believes to be right.

To this extent the quality of a person is determined by the loftiness and strength of what Steiner calls his 'moral imagination'.

It is the source from which springs the activity of the free spirit. It is for this reason that only people possessed of moral imagination are truly productive in a moral sense. Teachers of moral lessons, that is to say people who reel off moral precepts without the power to embody them in tangible notions, are morally unproductive.

Viewing in retrospect this fundamental work, of the content of which we have here given the barest indications which could never adequately take the place of the actual study of the book, Steiner says in his *Autobiography*:

My *Philosophy of Freedom* is based on experiences which consist in the reconciliation of the human consciousness with itself. Freedom is exercised in willing; it is experienced in feeling; it is recognized in thinking. But if this is to be achieved, living must not be allowed to be swallowed up in thinking.

Perhaps this will serve to make clear why Steiner throughout his life insisted on the need for live, not dead, thought as a condition for the understanding of his anthroposophy.

This period ends with the book: *Goethe's World View* (1897). On the side—as if to demonstrate his enormous capacity for work—he wrote the introductions to the works of Schopenhauer (1894–95) and Jean Paul (1897), which had been published in the Cottasche Bibliothek der Weltliteratur.

On his leaving Weimar in 1897, the annual report of the Goethe-Gesellschaft officially recognized his work at the Goethe-und-Schiller-Archiv in the following words: 'His work, which combined critical acumen with actual achievement, has gained the commendation of all those who are best qualified to judge. Thanks to his dedication, a wealth of orderly records, assembled in accordance with a uniform plan, is now available which will lead to a fuller appreciation, and enhance the standing, of Goethe as a scientist.' Steiner, now thirty-six, will doubtless have been pleased with this notice—albeit the 'official' Weimar circle neither remarked nor understood what he was in reality aiming at.

BERLIN 1897–1900

The Turning Point

My Weimar period ended when I was thirty-six. Already a year before this a profound change had begun to manifest itself in my way of thinking. At the time of my departure from Weimar it became a conscious experience. It was quite independent of the change in my circumstances, great though this was.

Throughout childhood and youth, throughout the Vienna and Weimar periods, Steiner was dogged by the same difficulty: that he could not experience the natural world with the same intensity as he did the ideal and the spiritual world. Whereas the life of the mind was an open book to him, and whereas he lived in his mind in a state of the highest alertness, in the natural world of shapes, colours, and sounds he was as it were a dreamer. Rudolf Steiner at first lacked the very thing that distinguishes a 'modern' youth who has grown up in the city streets: the over-alertness of the senses.

I experienced the greatest difficulty in observing and taking in the natural world. It was as though I was unable to infuse the mental experience into the organs of sense with sufficient energy to make what they experienced entirely one with my mind. From the beginning of my thirty-sixth year, all this changed completely. I found myself able to observe the objects, beings, and processes of the physical world with increased accuracy and penetration.

... There awoke in my mind an awareness of sensory objects that had never been there before.

He was aware that in the natural way this 'mental turning point' is completed, gradually and organically, in childhood.

What distinguishes Rudolf Steiner's development is that he did not undergo this process until much later in life. As far as concerned his relation to the external world he remained a child for longer. Having experienced this change so much later in life, it was in a state of full consciousness that he experienced it, and this was the positive aspect of such a late development.

> I observed that because people make the change from psychic activity in the spiritual world to the experience of the physical world at an early age, they end without fully grasping either the spiritual or the physical world. They instinctively intermingle the messages that objects convey to their senses with what the psyche experiences through the mind, which they then in part make use of in order to represent objects to themselves.

It is difficult to imagine what this 'mental turning point' must have been like. In a relatively short time the natural world, which until then had seemed to Steiner as if shrouded in mist, became revealed to him with a clarity and distinctness such as he had never before experienced. The mist dispersed, and the external world in all its colours and outlines lay before him, bathed in sunlight. 'The precision with which I was now able to observe sensory objects, and the way they penetrated my consciousness, opened up a new world for me.'

Obviously, his new relationship to the world around him reacted on Steiner's inner world. His mental life was given a boost, the main effect of which was seen in his relations with his fellow human beings:

> My powers of observation were directed towards observing, entirely objectively and as an object of contemplation, life as people live it. I scrupulously avoided criticising what people did, or allowing sympathy or antipathy to influence my

relationship with them; my aim was *simply to experience the effect on me of man as he is*. I soon discovered that this kind of observation of the world leads us into the realms of the spirit.

Only now did he feel that he was living in a world that was complete, and that he could move at will between his inner world and the external world. He now saw that 'true understanding of life' consists in experiencing the polarity of the internal and the external world, being aware of both these worlds with an equal degree of consciousness, and maintaining the balance between them. This is how he describes his new situation:

> This is a world full of enigmas. Knowledge seeks to reach the solution. But in most instances an attempt is made to pass off the thinking about a riddle as constituting its solution. But *thinking* does not solve problems. Thinking puts the mind on the right road to the solution. But the solution does not lie there.
>
> ...And so I told myself: the whole world, man apart, is an enigma, the enigma of the world; and *man himself is the solution*.

In many respects, the intellectual life of Berlin in 1897 was stratified. The imperial era of Wilhelm II had arrived. Wilhelm II had dismissed Bismarck, who was in retirement on his estates at Sachsenwald. But the great age of Alexander von Humboldt, Hegel, and Schleiermacher was still to some extent making its influence felt. No less a man than Herman Grimm, who was prominent in the activities of the Goethe-and-Schiller Archives at Weimar, occupied a chair at the university. It was an obvious step for Steiner to turn to Herman Grimm and through him seek the entrée to academic circles in Berlin. In Herman Grimm he made the acquaintance of that personality among the students of Goethe—Schröer apart—whose own life and fortunes were a

*Herman Grimm
(1828–1901)*

reminder of the great classical period of Weimar. Herman
Grimm was married to Gisela von Arnim, the daughter of
that Bettina von Arnim who, through Goethe's *Correspon-
dence with a Child*, formed the link between all students of
Goethe and Goethe's intimate circle. Rudolf Steiner saw in
Herman Grimm 'as it were an intellectual descendant of
Goethe', and naturally revered him. At Weimar, he recalls,
he had often felt that 'Intellectual distinction entered the
Archives with Herman Grimm whenever he appeared there.
From the time when, still in Vienna, I read his work on
Goethe, I felt myself powerfully attracted to the mind of this
man.' This is understandable, for Herman Grimm was like
the last evening rays of sunlight from that heyday of the
world of Goethe, a world which by the end of the nineteenth
century was otherwise as good as dead. 'Whenever Herman
Grimm was at the Archives, it seemed as if hidden threads
led back from them to Goethe.'

Nothing could have been more natural for Steiner than that, being in Berlin, he should seek to attach himself to him as much as possible and through him to share in the official intellectual life of Berlin. Herman Grimm would assuredly have been of great assistance to him. But this was the very thing that Steiner willed himself not to do.

While Steiner was still at Weimar, Herman Grimm, in a communicative mood that was rare for him, when they were lunching alone together at a hotel, expounded his thoughts on the 'history of the German imagination'. This discourse made a powerful impression upon Steiner, but he was at once aware of the abyss that separated him from Herman Grimm:

> I believed that I understood how supernatural spirituality works through men. The mind of this man was able to glimpse the creative spirit, but had no desire to apprehend its intrinsic life, remaining rather in that region where what is spiritual is experienced as imagination.

Otto Erich Hartleben (1864–1905)

Goethe's aversion to 'thinking about thinking', to exploring the objective nature of the thoughts and ideas that present themselves in the subjective arena of the human mind, was shared in an equal measure by Herman Grimm. Thus it was that Rudolf Steiner—not without an inner struggle—sought to ally himself to a quite different circle.

Since 1832, the year of Goethe's death, a 'literary magazine' had been appearing in Berlin under a variety of names and with a variety of publishers. Rudolf Steiner purchased this magazine. One of the conditions of purchase was that he should co-opt Otto Erich Hartleben as joint editor. Rudolf Steiner accepted this obligation, which did not in all respects make his task easier, as a 'decree of fate'. Principally for economic reasons, the *Magazin für Litteratur* at the same time became the organ of the Freie literarische Gesellschaft (Independent Literary Society), the revolutionary antagonist of the traditional Literarische Gesellschaft.

This was the human setting in which Rudolf Steiner now found himself at the age of thirty-six. The inner 'change' of the Weimar period now extended itself to his external life, giving it a new direction which could not have been more radically opposed to that of the Vienna and Weimar periods. Steiner chose for his new social world, not the formidable faculty of the University of Berlin, but the avant-garde of the Bohemians, whose like the capital of the German Empire had never seen.

It was as though he wished to put it to the test, whether his abundant inner life could withstand the most violent disruptive stresses to which life in *this world* would subject it. Shortly before his death he harked back to those 'Years of Trial' in Berlin.

The period from my departure from Weimar—1897—to the completion of my book *Christianity as Mystical Fact*—1902—is

Facsimile of Das Magazin

filled with this trial. Such trials are the obstacles decreed by fate (karma) which spiritual development has to surmount.

In an essay entitled 'Personalities in Rudolf Steiner's Berlin Circle Before the Turn of the Century', Emil Bock attempts by means of individual character sketches to convey the atmosphere of Rudolf Steiner's life at that time.

'...The sedate, cultivated bourgeoisie viewed with extreme moral indignation the circle that surrounded Otto Erich Hartleben. Anyone who frequented that circle was definitely not salon material. And so Rudolf Steiner had to choose between the two circles. Although he gave offence all round by doing so, he joined the odd men out, eccentrics, idlers, night owls, and outsiders of society. But life there was truly colourful, there was bustle and activity. To illustrate the style that reigned there, I will begin with a small anecdote: Otto Erich Hartleben was not fond of staying at home of an

Dramaturgiſche Blätter

Erſcheint jeden Sonnabend.

Organ des deutſchen Bühnen-Vereins.
(Beiblatt zum Magazin für Litteratur.)

Preis 1,50 Mark vierteljährlich. Einzelnummer 15 Pfg.

Herausgegeben von **Rudolf Steiner.** — Redaktion: Berlin W 30, Habsburgerstraße 11 I.

Beſtellungen werden von jeder Buchhandlung, jedem Poſtamt (Nr. 2086 a der Poſtzeitungsliſte), ſowie vom Verlage des „Magazins" entgegengenommen.

1. Jahrgang. **Berlin und Weimar, den 21. Mai 1898.** Nr. 20.

Unbefugter Nachdruck wird auf Grund der Geſetze und Verträge verfolgt.

Das Wiener Theater.
Hiſtoriſches und Modernes.
Von
W. Fred.
(Fortſetzung.)

Der Erfolg dieſes Shakeſpeare-Zyklus muß ganz ungeheuer geweſen ſein. Während noch in den unmittelbar vorhergegangenen Jahren über ſehr ſchlechten Beſuch des Burgtheaters ſelbſt am Sonntag geklagt wurde, war zum Shakeſpeare-Zyklus an allen Abenden das Haus bis ...

wie die Rezenſenten damals über Ibſen urteilten, was ſie von ihm erwarten zu müſſen glaubten und wie ſie ſeine dramatiſchen Abſichten auffaßten. Ludwig Speidel*) erklärt, daß das Stück gar keinen nordiſchen Charakter habe. Malitiös weiſt er Ibſen neben George Sand einen Platz an. Er erſcheint als eleganter Geiſt franzöſiſcher Salons. Nach Darſtellung des dramatiſchen Konflikts heißt es in dieſem Feuilleton: „Nun (. . . zur Löſung des Knotens . . .) gilt es, ein dichtender Nordlandsrecke zu ſein, ein tragiſcher Poet, der vor der äußerſten Konſequenz nicht zurückſchreckt. Henrik Ibſen hält dieſe Probe nicht aus . . . . ." Zum Schluſſe meinte ...

evening. But neither, when he was sitting around in his boozers, was he very enthusiastic about going home. It was always broad daylight before he set out for home. It was small wonder that he did not get out of bed until the afternoon. One morning he was making his way through the Tiergarten as usual. There was someone lying asleep on a bench. Hartleben studied him carefully and saw that it was a good friend of his, the poet Peter Hille. He went up to him, shook him awake, and said: "Peter, this won't do, camping out in the Tiergarten in the damp. You have still so much to give humanity. Now, do go and find yourself a room." When Peter had roused himself, off the two of them trotted. They had to wait for full daylight, and until then they whiled away their time in a cafe frequented by night cabmen. When the house doors had been opened the two of them went from house to house in the quarter around the Nollendorfplatz, looking for a cheap room. After a long search they found a room on the 5th floor of a house, and already Peter Hille was dreaming of editing a journal of world renown from here. He wanted to be off at once to fetch the bag which contained his collected works on scraps of paper and which he had left with some friends. Otto Erich paid two months' rent in advance. Both were happy: Otto Erich had done a good deed and Peter Hille had the opportunity at least for a time to lead a regular life. Next morning, at about the same time, Hartleben was walking the same way through the Tiergarten. The only difference was that it was raining. Peter Hille was lying on the bench, just as he had been the day before. Hartleben was furious and gave him a piece of his mind. Peter Hille asked him: "Look, have you got the address?" And Hartleben had to admit that he had forgotten it too.'

It would be wrong to conclude from such anecdotes that this circle consisted entirely of unfortunate beings who had come to grief in the world. The genius of many of those who gathered in this Berlin circle about the turn of the century far outweighed the human weaknesses. Otto Erich Hartleben and Peter Hille, and many others besides, were well above average. Rudolf Steiner developed a particularly cordial relationship with the poet Ludwig Jacobowski, the founder of the association known as 'Die Kommenden' ('The Coming Generation'). In this circle, young artists read their first compositions. Lectures on many subjects made these gatherings a source of knowledge. Steiner frequently played a part. The discussions which followed gave the audiences a deeper insight into the subject matter.

> The evening ended with unconstrained social interaction. Ludwig Jacobowski was the centre of the constantly expanding circle. Everyone loved this amiable personality, who was so fertile in ideas, and who in this company disclosed a rich vein of cultivated humour ... This was a personality whose soul was rooted in inner tragedy.

On 2 December 1900, three months after Nietzsche (who died on 25 August), Jacobowski died at the age of thirty of meningitis. Steiner was deeply affected. He undertook the task of reciting the funeral oration for his friend, and thereafter acted as trustee of his literary remains.

Rudolf Steiner contracted a particularly close friendship with another outstanding personality: John Henry Mackay, Scottish born but since 1898 'Berliner by choice'. To the cultivated citizens of the capital of the Empire Mackay was a disturbing phenomenon. He had written a novel *The Anarchists*, edited the works of the controversial 'individualist' Stirner, and defended with the utmost conviction his philosophy of life, for which he coined the term 'individualistic anarchism'. Reason enough for many people to regard him with the gravest suspicion. Steiner had made his acquaintance while still at Weimar—and had found him 'a thoroughly congenial personality', whom he learned to esteem.

Around Mackay there was an aura of a wider world. 'Externally and internally, his demeanour bespoke experience of the world. He had spent periods in England and in America. All this was tinged with his boundless amiability.'

There may have been a passing phase during which Steiner assumed that the resemblance between his own exposition of ethical individualism in his *Philosophy of Freedom* and Mackay's individualistic anarchism was closer than it really was. However that may be, this period of friendship with Mackay was likewise the period of his decided and aggressive assertion of the absolute autonomy of the free man and his absolute rejection of all external authority. In this period he was spiritually in jeopardy:

About that time, around 1898, this purely ethical individualism had as it were dragged my soul down into an abyss. Something that was purely and intrinsically human was about to become externalised. The esoteric was about to be turned aside into the exoteric.

Steiner overcame this very real temptation, one might almost say this spiritual trial. His subsequent career proves this once and for all. Reading what he wrote about his friend John Henry Mackay, we have the feeling that we are observing Steiner's own spiritual struggle:

> Mackay's refined perceptions derived from the fundamental sense of the enormous responsibility of the personality to itself. Meek, submissive natures seek for a Godhead, an ideal that they can revere and worship. They are unable to abrogate worth to themselves and look to something outside themselves to confer it upon them. Proud natures only acknowledge in themselves that which they have created out of themselves ... They are therefore sensitive to all external interference with their lives. Their ego seeks to build its own world, in which it can develop without hindrance. It is only through this reverence for his own personality that a man comes to esteem the ego in others. Mackay's is a superior, self-confident nature. And he who with such earnestness plumbs the depths of his own soul is stirred by passions and desires of which he who knows not freedom can form no conception...

These words could only have been written by one who had himself gazed into those depths.

John Mackay was a witness when on 31 October 1899 at the Registrar's Office at Berlin-Friedenau 'the friendship with Anna Eunike culminated in a civil marriage'. Anna Eunike had moved to Berlin already before Steiner left Weimar. When he followed her shortly afterwards, he first of all took a place of his own, on Karlsbad, near the Potsdam bridge, but it was only for a short time that he experienced the 'whole wretched business of living in a place of one's own'. Thereafter he rejoined the Eunikes.

*John Henry Mackay
(1864–1933)*

Statements to the contrary notwithstanding, this marriage never ended in divorce. After several years' separation from Steiner, Anna Steiner-Eunike died on 19 March 1911. Shortly before her death she told her daughter Wilhelmine: 'Those years with Rudolf Steiner were the best of my life.'

Rudolf Steiner's life in Berlin was greatly enriched by the teaching work that he undertook at the Arbeiter-Bildungsschule (Workers' Educational Institute) founded by Wilhelm Liebknecht. With studied indifference to the political aims of the board of governors of this school, he placed his knowledge and his gift for teaching at the service of the school for workers. This was a time when many workers who were seeking for self-improvement were pursuing education and knowledge with enthusiastic resolve. Frequently misinterpreted though it may have been, the slogan 'Knowledge is power' nevertheless did epitomize the striving for emancipation of a proletariat eager for human freedom.

> It became my noble duty to instruct mature men and women of the working class. For there were few young people among the students. I told the board that if I undertook teaching duties I would teach history according to my own ideas about the development of humanity, not in accordance with the marxist principles currently in vogue in social democratic circles. They still wished for my services as a teacher.

Without thought of self and without identifying himself with the materialistic philosophy of the governors, Steiner gave his services. The subject matter that he taught at this workers' school ranged from the history of the Middle Ages, the French Revolution, and modern times to the 'growth of the universe and the social life of animals' and the 'anatomy of man'.

There was as yet no eight-hour day or forty-hour week. A working day of 10–12 hours was normal. So much greater was the effort of will made by those proletarians who from 9 to 11 in the evening—often indeed until 12 o'clock—pursued their studies with burning zeal, despite the poorest educational basis imaginable.

Rudolf Steiner, who taught up to five evenings a week, had up to 200 students on some of his courses. In addition, in January 1900 he inaugurated courses in public speaking, at which workers learned to express themselves before gatherings. Emil Bock discovered a document dating from this period which bore the title 'Grete Lenz, a girl from Berlin' and which conveys something of the atmosphere of these courses in public speaking.

'When I heard about the Workers' Educational Institute I went along to the Engel-Ufer and enrolled. I had intended to read political economy, but I found the subject so boring that one lecture was enough for me. And it must have been very fatiguing, for in front of me and behind me there were a number of workers who had fallen asleep and were snoring so loudly that the lecturer was repeatedly startled and almost came to a stop. I found Rudolf Steiner more inspiring. He taught the working men and women the art of public speaking. Every member of the class was allowed to go up on the platform and speak on some subject, and Dr Steiner corrected the speaker whenever necessary. I was often astonished at how skilfully and correctly those simple people spoke.'

The culminating point of these activities came when on 17 June 1900 Steiner was invited to address as chief speaker a purely working-class audience of 7000 type-setters and printers on the occasion of the Gutenberg Quincentenary in a great Berlin circus. He performed this task—without a loudspeaker!—and was given an enthusiastic reception. Which proves how wrong it would be to think of Rudolf Steiner around 1900 as a 'withdrawn private tutor'.

*Ludwig Jacobowski
(1868–1900)*

Here is how he himself summed up the situation of the working class at that time:

> I have the impression that if a larger number of disinterested persons had interested themselves in the working-class movement and had shown understanding for the proletariat, the movement would have taken a quite different course. But the workers were left to live their lives out within their own class while the other classes remained inside their own circles. This was the period in which the upper classes lost their community sense and in which egoism and the wild excesses of the competitive spirit spread far and wide ... Gradually, all communication between the different classes ceased.

Steiner continued his work at this institute until the beginning of 1905. Excessive outside commitments, and intrigues inside the politically motivated board, made it impossible for him to continue to work there.

In these years Steiner associated himself with a totally different circle, the so-called 'Friedrichshagener'. Bruno Wille, and Haeckel's friend Wilhelm Bölsche, set the tone here. They founded an 'independent academy', in which the liberal theologian Theodor Kappstein played an active part, and the influential 'Giordano Bruno Federation'—the latter was dominated by a central theme, with which it sought to come to grips: Monism. Different though this circle was from that of the Independent Literary Society, of 'The Coming Generation', or of the Workers' Educational Institute, it is still the same old story. Rudolf Steiner contributes all his powers to the human and spiritual relationships in which he finds himself involved. He plays an active part, meets recognition and opposition, is one of them and yet remains an often welcome guest—and a stranger. For what lies nearest his heart he finds neither understanding nor acceptance.

Rudolf Steiner as a teacher at the Workers' Educational Institute, 1901

This brings us to his classical lecture to the Giordano Bruno Federation on 8 October 1902: 'Monism and Theosophy.'

This lecture acted like a bomb. It was really too much for the good folk who, taking Haeckel's 'world enigmas', had pieced together from it a nice, homespun Monism according to which unity was achieved by the sacrifice of the spiritual wealth of the world. A Monism which gave equal recognition to both the material and the spiritual aspects of the world was over the heads of the majority of his audience. They had not the mental calibre to understand this 'bombshell' of an idea. And so once again Rudolf Steiner stood alone in the midst of a circle which was bound to him by ties of human friendship. He had shown his colours, his position was clear. He had knocked at the door, which, once open, was now closed against him. If he was not to lapse into silence, he must find other ways and other people. And he would not, nor could he, remain silent.

FROM THEOSOPHY TO ANTHROPOSOPHY

Steiner's avowal of his belief in theosophy, in theosophy, that is, as he wished it to be understood, by no means led to the severance of his relations with the various circles in Berlin in which he had hitherto been active. It is true that in various circles he was viewed with greater reserve, but he continued to receive many invitations to deliver lectures and courses. To The Coming Generation alone, up to April 1903 he had delivered twenty-seven lectures on the theme:

> From Zarathustra to Nietzsche. The story of the development of Man as reflected in world philosophies, from the earliest oriental times up to the present, or Anthroposophy.

This is the first time that he used the word which he was later to apply to his own brand of spiritual science: Anthroposophy. It had already been used as a word and as a designation by Immanuel Hermann, the son of Johann Gottlieb Fichte. One of Rudolf Steiner's tutors at the University of Vienna, Robert Zimmermann, the rigorously systematic aesthetical theorist, had taken the word Anthroposophy as the title for his standard work on aesthetics. But it was first given its essential significance through its association with the life work of Rudolf Steiner.

But his first steps along this road led him to the Theosophical Society. He had already made a start, privately, some time before. Shortly after he had given up editing the *Magazin für Litteratur* he had received, arising out of the writing of his work on Nietzsche, an invitation to speak in September 1900 at two of the weekly lecture evenings given by Count and Countess Brockdorff at the Theosophical

Library, Kaiser-Friedrichstrasse 54a. A few weeks previously, on 25 August, Friedrich Nietzsche had been released
from his grievous suffering. He was the subject of the first
lecture. This was followed eight days later by 'Goethe's
secret Revelation'.

These two lectures appealed to this audience, the majority
of whom were theosophists. And Rudolf Steiner had found a
forum where, following his own spiritual bent, he could lay
the foundations of his future work. In the winter of 1900–
1901 he delivered a course of 27 lectures, the subject matter
of which later appeared in print in a book entitled *Mysticism
at the Dawn of the Modern Age, and its Relation to Modern
World Philosophy.*

In the winter of 1901/02 he delivered to the same audience
in the same meeting-place a further 25 lectures, the content
of which he brought together in the book entitled: *Christianity as Mystical Fact.* Both these works still form part of the
essential introductory reading for the study of anthroposophy. But in both these works it is made plain that Rudolf
Steiner deliberately takes his stand, not on oriental theosophy, but on the intellectual life of Europe and the con-
tinuity of that which has given the West substance and
strength: Christianity.

> *No one was left in any doubt* that in the Theosophical Society I
> would present only the results of my own insight. For I said as
> much at every opportunity. And when the German Branch of
> the Theosophical Society was founded in Berlin in the presence
> of Annie Besant and I was elected to the post of General
> Secretary, I had to leave the foundation meeting because I had
> to deliver one of the lectures I was giving to a non-theosophical
> audience about the intellectual development of man, and I had
> expressly added to the title: 'a study in anthroposophy'. Annie
> Besant was aware that under this title I was at the time giving
> utterance to what I had to say about the spiritual world.

When I went to London for a theosophical congress, a leading personality said to me that my book *Mysticism* contained the truth about theosophy. This satisfied me. For I had merely described the results of my own spiritual insight; and these found acceptance in the Theosophical Society. There was no longer any reason why I should not present spiritual knowledge to theosophical audiences, the only ones which at that time had dedicated themselves to it, *in my own chosen way.* I did not subscribe to any sectarian dogma; I remained someone who expressed what he believed himself to have the power to express about his own experiences of the spiritual world.

At one of these lectures, Marie von Sivers was among the audience. She it was whom fate had chosen to take over and guide with a firm hand the German Branch of the Theosophical Society, founded just after I had started my lectures. I was now able within this branch to develop my anthroposophical views before a constantly increasing public.

From the very first day of his active participation in this work there was evidence of a fundamental difference of both method and content between Rudolf Steiner's tenets and what Helena Petrovna Blavatsky and Annie Besant propagated as 'theosophy'. Steiner accepted nothing, absolutely nothing derived from occult tradition, unless he had rediscovered it for himself through his own seeking. But in his search he would not admit of the least inaccuracy but demanded the same rigorous discipline as has become the rule in all other fields of western scientific research. It is true that in the years immediately after 1902 Steiner did employ the terminology of oriental theosophy, albeit with restraint, in order to make himself understood, but in the years that followed he sought to replace the oriental terms by words more in tune with the modern consciousness.

The all-important difference, which led to the final break with the Indian-Anglo-Saxon theosophy in 1912/13, lay in

Steiner's attitude to Christianity. For all that he rejected, at times radically, the historic forms and dogmas of the churches, throughout his life he saw in Jesus Christ and the 'Events of Golgotha' the central occurrence in the history of the world and humanity—we need only call to mind his conversations with Father Wilhelm Neumann in Vienna round about 1886. This point of view was alien to theosophists like Helena Petrovna Blavatsky, Annie Besant, and H.S. Olcott. Their supreme ideal was a general synthesis of all religions and their equally valid truths, and this they hoped to achieve by an understanding tolerance.

They neither understood nor acknowledged the *unique* nature of the appearance on earth of Christ the Son of God in the person of the Man Jesus of Nazareth. Instead of this, Annie Besant proclaimed the boy Krishnamurti as the reincarnation of Christ.

But after 1906 the Society, on the leadership of which I had not the slightest influence, was invaded by practices which suggested an outgrowth of spiritualism and which made it necessary for me to stress more and more that that part of the Society of which I was the leader had absolutely nothing to do with such matters. The ultimate outcome of these practices was that a Hindu boy maintained that he was the person in whom Christ was to be reincarnated in a new life on earth. A special branch of the Theosophical Society was founded with the object of propagating this absurdity, under the name of the Star of the East. My friends and I simply could not admit the members of this Star of the East into membership of the German branch, which was what they desired and what above all Annie Besant, as president of the Theosophical Society, had intended. And, because we were unable to do this, in 1913 we were barred from the Theosophical Society. We were compelled to found the Anthroposophical Society as an independent entity.

Thus it was a specific event that brought about the severance of the connection with the Theosophical Society. But the division was there from the very moment that they started to work together. The schism occurred as it were at the frontier between those who did and those who did not believe that the phenomenon of Christ was of quite special significance for humanity.

On the other hand, Rudolf Steiner had a high regard for the truth that was at the heart of the ancient wisdom of the Orient. However, he was convinced that there was nothing in the riches of the traditional wisdom of Asia that could give it the power to overcome the scientific materialism that sets the intellectual tone for the civilized world today. The power to do this resides in the mind of the West itself. The nameless 'Master' who had said: 'Only he can overcome the dragon who can slip into the dragon's skin,' pointed the way.

Modern science is not human development on the wrong

Marie von Sivers, later
Rudolf Steiner's
second wife
(around 1910)

track, as for instance the atomic physicist Jordan teaches, but the human intellect's road to Golgotha, by which through the spiritualization of his thinking man will achieve his resurrection and celebrate his Easter. The power and substance of the theosophy founded on the principle works of Helena Petrovna Blavatsky, *Isis unveiled* and *The Secret Doctrine*, lacks the means to achieve this. To her own time she meant something, and she put many a seeker after spiritual truth in the age of materialism on the right road. But all in all the increasing ease of access to oriental wisdom is for the European a temptation not to follow his right road to his goal. Think of the many and various yoga systems with which the West of today is inundated. We in the West have every

Helena Petrovna Blavatsky (1831–1891) and Henry Steel Olcott (1832–1907)

reason to acknowledge with true reverence the profundity and the loftiness of spirit of that sacred Hindu scripture the Bhagavadgita, the Upanishads, the Vedanta, and many more. But they can as little solve our problems as can the works of Confucius, Lao-tzu, Ramakrishna, Sri Aurobindo, or Sarvepalli Radhakrishnan.

In this connection it is to be noted that the theosophical movement had as its headquarters at Adyar near Madras and drew primarily on oriental sources. Rudolf Steiner revered the East, but did not look to it for a solution of the problems of the West.

West–East Aphorisms

'The Oriental once experienced the world within himself, and in his spiritual life he now hears its echoes; the Westerner is at the start of his experience and has set out to find his way in the world. If he wished to become a yogi, a Westerner would have to become an out-and-out egoist, for nature has conferred on him that consciousness of self that to the Oriental was no more than a dream experience; if the yogi, like the Westerner, had sought to discover himself in the world, he would have taken his dream experience with him into unconscious sleep and would have been like a drowned soul.

'The Oriental spoke of the natural world as an illusion in which there lived on a lower plane that which his soul perceived in the completeness of reality as spirit. The Westerner speaks of the ideal world as an illusion in which there lives in a shadowy form that which he experiences with his senses in the fullness of reality as nature. That which to the oriental is *maya* is to the Westerner the fullness of reality. That which to the Westerner is intellectual ideology was to the Oriental reality with creative powers of its own. When the Oriental of today finds in his spiritual reality the power to give being to *maya*, and when the Westerner finds that in the reality of nature there is life which can perceive the active principle in his ideology; then East and West will understand each other.

'The Oriental is not concerned with *proving* things. He

Rudolf Steiner and Annie Besant (1847–1933) Munich, 1907

knows what he is aware of as reality by contemplating it. And what a person knows he does not *prove*. The Westerner always demands *proofs*. He apprehends reality from its outward reflection and struggles with it using thought, and it is by thinking that he interprets it. But what must be interpreted must also be *proved*. When the Westerner redeems the life of reality from proof, then the Oriental will understand him. When at the end of the Westerner's preoccupation with truth the Oriental finds his unproved dreams of reality, the Westerner will welcome him as a fellow worker in the furtherance of human progress who is able to achieve what he himself is incapable of.

(Words written on the occasion of the West-East Congress in Vienna in 1922. In German in: *Der Goetheanumgedanke. Gesammelte Aufsätze 1921–1925.*)

ANTHROPOSOPHY

'In the period which now follows it will be hard to disentangle my life story from the history of the anthroposophical movement.' These words of Rudolf Steiner's apply to the two decades which start about 1905 and end with his death in 1925. His spiritual and physical activity was unceasing. He created anthroposophy as a spiritual science, as an art, and as a social motivation and his aim was to establish it in human minds and human societies.

His anthroposophical activity can be divided into four phases. Each is a preparation for the next, they overlap in time but can be clearly distinguished:

1. The evolution of anthroposophy, 1902–1909;
2. Art, 1910–1916;
3. The period in which the communities were established, 1919–1923;
4. From the 'Christmas Conference' to the death of Rudolf Steiner, 1924–1925.

The Development of Anthroposophy as a Spiritual Science (1902–1909)

From the very moment that the German branch of the Theosophical Society was founded I regarded a journal as an essential. And so Marie von Sivers and I founded the monthly journal *Lucifer*. The name was of course in no way linked with the spiritual power to which I later applied the same name as a designation for the force opposed to Ahriman. The name was simply intended to mean the 'Bearer of Light'.

The number of readers increased rapidly, and later the Vienna journal *Gnosis* was absorbed. The name was then changed to *Lucifer-Gnosis*. Steiner was supported in this work by Marie von Sivers.

> It was Marie von Sivers who made all this possible, for she not only contributed to the full extent of her means in a material sense but devoted all her energies to anthroposophy. The conditions in which we worked at the beginning were as primitive as can be imagined. I wrote most of the copy for *Lucifer*. Marie von Sivers dealt with the correspondence. When a number had been got out we prepared the wrappers and addressed and stamped them, and took them to the post in a laundry basket.

Lucifer-Gnosis flourished, the number of subscribers increased—but in spite of this in 1908 it was necessary to cease publication. Excess of work, mainly owing to the con-

Programme of the series of lectures in Helsinki, 1912

stantly increasing number of lecture engagements, at first mostly in Germany but later throughout Europe, made it impossible for Steiner to continue to edit a regular monthly journal.

> 'And this brought about the odd situation that a journal that was gaining subscribers with every issue had to cease publication because the editor was overburdened with work.'

Berlin continued to be the centre of activity. He continued to reside there—at 17 Motzstrasse—until after the end of the First World War. It was from there that he set out on his countless journeys. (See the Chronology at the end of the book). It was in Berlin that the Philosophical-Theosophical (later, Philosophical-Anthroposophical) Publishing House was established. This was under the management of Marie von Sivers. It was not until 1923 that the headquarters at Motzstrasse were relinquished and the publishing business was transferred to Dornach.

The articles in *Lucifer* and in *Lucifer-Gnosis*, and the lecture series, provided the original material out of which the standard works on anthroposophy were evolved.

Theosophy (1904)

The first standard work in which Rudolf Steiner brought anthroposophy to the notice of the public forms a link with Fichte: 'This dogma presupposes a new inner organ of sense which opens up a new world and with which ordinary people are not equipped at all ... Imagine a world in which everyone is born blind, so that objects, and the relationships between them, are recognized only through the sense of touch. Go among these people and speak to them of colours and other phenomena that only light and the faculty of sight can reveal. You will be talking to them about nothing, and the best thing is that they tell you so; for in this way you will soon be made aware of your error, and, unless you can open their eyes, stop wasting words.' (Fichte, 1813)

Rudolf Steiner was made aware of the spiritual blindness of his generation and believed with every fibre of his being that it was possible to heal the blind. He did not become silent. He tried with every means at his disposal to open the spiritual eyes of his contemporaries. His *Theosophy* is his first direct attempt to open the eyes of the spirit of modern man through the medium of a book, no longer merely by speech, by lectures, and by personal commitment.

The first edition is dedicated to the 'Spirit of Giordano Bruno', the man who spiritually was born before his time and was condemned to death by the Church in 1600.

Many of the thoughts that Steiner expressed in his book are to be found in a more or less clear form in Bruno. One such is the idea of repeated life on earth.

Theosophy considers man and the world as a trinity. Body, soul, and spirit are formed from three world spheres. A human being of sound mind is aware of himself as a self-contained personality. Nevertheless he belongs to three spheres of existence:

1. The body to the physical or natural world
2. The soul to the intellectual or soul world
3. The spirit to the spiritual world

To the spiritually blind person only the first plane of existence, the physical world, is real. The intellectual or soul world is experienced as a world of shadows. The spiritual world is without reality for him. Against this, Steiner portrays the three spheres, each of which, for all the differences between them, is individually alive and active. One cannot imagine the human body in isolation without a physical world, and just as little can one imagine the subjective experience of the soul without an objective intellectual or soul world, or the individual spirit without a spiritual world. The three worlds are differentiated in and around the human being on many planes.

Theosophy was written in order to serve as an 'introduction to the knowledge of the supernatural world and the destiny of man'.

The list of contents gives a clear indication of the arrangement of the subject matter:

> The Essential Nature of the Human Being
> Destiny and the Reincarnation of the Spirit
> The Three Worlds
> (Physical World, Soul World, Spiritual World)
> The Path to Knowledge

> This is not a book to be read in the way that is customary today. In a certain sense the reader has to *study* every page, sometimes even every sentence. (From the preface.)

> This book sets out to describe some of the features of the supernatural world. Whoever is concerned only with the senses will look on this description as a phantasy without substance. But he who is searching for the road that leads out of the natural world will at once realize that human life acquires value and meaning only through insight into another world.

These sentences sketch out the spiritual journey which will bring perception of the world and human destiny into union in Steiner's sense. The quest for knowledge of the world may serve as the motive of intellectual curiosity but it is of no avail when it comes to acquiring insight into human destiny—whatever its contribution to technical invention. For Steiner it is essential that no pronouncement shall be made that is not based on reality as an experience. It might be said that what he aims at in his philosophy of the world is 'spiritual realism'.

The author describes nothing to which he cannot bear witness as the result of experience, the kind of experience that can be gained in this field. He proposes to describe only the things that in this sense he has experienced.

Those who knew Rudolf Steiner in his lifetime will be able to confirm that he is entitled to say these words about himself:

I will never say anything about spiritual matters that I do not know from *direct spiritual experience*. This is my guiding star. And this has enabled me to see through every illusion. (From a letter.)

The core of *Theosophy* is the chapter on Destiny and the Reincarnation of the Spirit. In a few pages the oldest human doctrine, which to a great extent still dominates the East today, is restated in western thought forms. This is done without making any reference to the past. Even Lessing, who was the first man in modern times to put forward this doctrine in a spirit of enquiry, in his *Education of the Human Race*, is not quoted in support of this theme. Without borrowing or seeking support from earlier authorities, Steiner gives an account of his own spiritual experience:

The human spirit must be reincarnated again and again; and the human being is governed by the law that he brings the fruits of his former life with him into the next one. The soul lives in the present. But this life in the present is not independent of the former life. The spirit that has been reincarnated brings its destiny with it from earlier incarnations. And this destiny rules his life. The impressions that the soul receives, the desires that are satisfied, the joys and sorrows that it experiences, depend on its actions in previous incarnations. The body is subject to the laws of heredity; the soul is subject to the destiny that it has itself created. This self-created destiny of man is called his karma. And the spirit is subject to the law of reincarnation.

> The spirit is eternal; in corporeal existence, birth and death alternate in accordance with the laws of the physical world; the life of the soul, which is governed by destiny, provides the cohesion between the two during a life on earth.

Rudolf Steiner's activities provide an abundance of concrete examples, with which he underpinned his doctrine. In 1924 alone, the last year in which his health allowed him to lecture, he undertook more than 60 'karma meditations'. These are replete with warnings not to try to get to the root of the interrelationships between two different lives on earth by indulging in intellectual subtleties. With irony, but in deep earnestness he was wont to visit his wrath on those who frivolously fabricated interrelationships between lives on earth. For him, only genuine spiritual experiences counted as the gaining of insight into earlier lives on earth. Even these should be used with the utmost caution in relating one case to another. But there are certain fundamental laws, such as:

> Someone who is in the habit of lying, or is inclined to make assumptions lightly will be a frivolous person in a later incarnation, for what we think, how we think, and our attitude to the truth, in short everything that is inherent in this incarnation, will be the yardstick for our behaviour in the next incarnation.

Throughout his life Steiner furnished many examples of the working of destiny, and of how what was the seed in one life must needs bear fruit in the next and following lives. Selfless love creates joy, which in the third incarnation blossoms out as a naturally open-hearted disposition. From hate and antipathy is born suffering, which produces folly and a stunted intellectual life in the third incarnation. In this sense the karma is bound by iron laws. But by education and self-tuition it can be made subject to regulation. Just as a river has its natural course which can be regulated by human intervention, so man has the opportunity and the freedom to influence the course of his own destiny.

This doctrine of reincarnation and karma is, in association with Christology, at the heart of anthroposophy. Rudolf Steiner was wholly taken up with the belief that this idea could give sense and purpose to western man, and hence to humanity.

> Just as once the time was ripe for the acceptance of the Copernican world philosophy, so the time has now come to inculcate into humanity at large the doctrine of reincarnation and karma.

Christian Morgenstern, Steiner's pupil, has in a diary the following entry dated 1911, which points in the same direction:

> The doctrine of reincarnation has been in circulation for a long time. But for a while it had to be thrust into a corner—the whole of European civilization derives from this neglect. Now this cycle has run its course, and reincarnation can return to the main stream of western development, bringing with it immeasurable blessings; two thousand years after Christ's time on earth, in a way that is new, and totally different than ever before, it will once again enrich, enlighten, and redeem mankind.

In *Theosophy* Steiner for the first time describes the fourfold, or sevenfold, nature of man; of this description we will now offer a brief synopsis.

In nature, three steps lead up to man: mineral, plant, animal. These three natural realms are manifestations of three spheres of existence, to which also man belongs. Consider together and individually:

> a rock-crystal
> a rose in bloom
> a startled deer.

Let these three natural objects work on you. The rock-crystal typifies the mineral world. It occupies space, but has no life. It consists of its components in juxtaposition; chemically speaking its constituents are the elements silicon and oxygen (SiO_2) and it is constructed in accordance with the laws of physics. It is hexagonal.

The rose represents the vegetable world. While it too occupies space, this space is constantly changing its shape. It has life, which is manifested in time in a succession of states: seed, shoot, blossom, and fruit.

The deer, like any other animal, occupies three spheres. Like the mineral it has its spatial body, which remains as a carcass when life ends. Like a plant it develops in a temporal dimension: embryo, fawn, mature deer. Its life is bounded by conception and death. A third element, lacking to minerals and plants, is added: vital force, the capacity to experience desire and aversion, the instincts.

In man there is a fourth element, the ego, which has the power to think, to feel, and to will.

Since the human being has a body, which in death becomes a corpse, he belongs to the mineral world. This Steiner calls his physical body. In that he is a being living in the time dimension, in which growth, propagation, metabolism, circulation occur, the human being resembles the plants. This second element, which corresponds to what Aristotle calls the vegetative soul, this system of life-shaping forces he calls the ethereal body. As a being possessing desires and urged on by passion, experiencing desire and aversion, man is related to the animals. This 'animal soul' in Aristotle's sense he calls the astral body. The fourth element, which makes man what he is, which distinguishes him from the animals, and whereby he is endowed with power to act as a spirit among spirits, is the ego.

Note that there is no conflict between this description of

the human being as made up from four elements and the trichotomy of body, soul, and spirit. It differentiates between that part of the body which draws its substance from the mineral world and returns to it on death and that part which constitutes life and whose nature is non-natural, super-natural, that is to say ethereal.

The use of the term astral body to describe the soul will at first jar on those at least who are unfamiliar with the works of Paracelsus, Jakob Boehme, etc. Steiner's reasons for not jettisoning this mystical term may well be linked with the dependence of animal and human life on astral influences (in some sort a justification of astrology). Steiner differentiates further between the various planes on which the human mind is operative within the astral body:

> the lower astral body (linked with the instinct to feed
> and propagate)
> the sentient soul
> the intellectual soul
> the consciousness-soul.

The human ego, refining and changing the three lower elements, predisposes them to become higher elements leading on beyond the ego and forging links with the Divine.

The final section of *Theosophy* has the title: The Path of Knowledge—and this introduces another central tenet of anthroposophy, without the understanding of which every-thing else would be left hanging in the air.

Someone who seeks to base his philosophy of the world on spiritual perceptions must bear within himself the certainty that these perceptions are not merely subjective in character. He must possess the faculty of distinguishing illusions, hal-lucinations, and phantasies of all kinds from reality, treating them in just the same way as a person for whom only the natural world has meaning needs to treat his life experiences, if he is to retain his spiritual health. If a natural scientist needs a thorough training in method if he is to achieve results in his chosen field, how much more does a spiritual scientist like Rudolf Steiner need constant methodical spiritual training and practice if he is to achieve spiritual objectivity. Flights of phantasy, a tendency to self-deception, auto-suggestion, have to be seen for what they are and overcome. This explains why in all the occult disciplines of the past 'the path of knowledge' leads through 'purging', through 'purification' of the human soul before there can be any question of enlightenment. Immediately after the publication of *Theosophy*, Steiner turned his attention to this other main theme. He dealt with the subject in a series of articles, of which the first appeared in 1904 and which were finally published in book form in 1909: *How to Know Higher Worlds.*

How to Know Higher Worlds (1904–1909)

There is a body of literature from the Indian theosophical tradition which contains advice on training in the occult. But in the West as far as we know there is nothing comparable to Steiner's second standard work on anthroposophy. Oriental occultists at the time actually regarded this publication as a 'betrayal of the mysteries'.

'In every human being faculties lie dormant by the exercise of which he can gain knowledge of higher spheres.' Thoughts and words like these break down the tradition going back for millennia according to which the 'hidden knowledge' can live only in the custody of shielded esoteric circles. Rudolf Steiner starts from the opposite assumption. For him this is the end of the age in which a small circle of informed initiates, living in strict isolation from the rest of mankind more or less in a state of dream-like ignorance, sought to direct history by drawing on sources of hidden knowledge. 'The time has come,' says the man with the lamp in Goethe's esoteric fable. The time has come. Rudolf Steiner was motivated by the same impulse.

Everyone today must quite freely open up his conscious mind to spiritual truths and journey by way of the sciences and the knowledge of the natural world that they reveal to him, and which he accepts, and so attain knowledge of the world of the soul and the spirit. But this requires discipline, and practice. This discipline begins on the 'path of reverence'. Unless the feeling of respect, devotion, veneration is cultivated, there will be no soil in which inward growth can be nurtured. Cynicism, mockery, fault-finding are enemies of more fully matured powers. It is not blank wonder that is meant, such as may be of great benefit to children, but 'reverence for truth and knowledge'.

> Experience shows that those people bear themselves best who have learned to venerate where veneration is due. And it is due whenever it comes from the depths of the heart.
>
> And feelings are to the soul what nourishment is to the body that it feeds ... Veneration, respect, devotion are the nourishment of the soul that keeps it healthy and strong: above all, strengthened for the activity of knowing.

It may be said that even for one who is by no means inclined to become a 'scholar of the spirit' this book can be a veritable compendium of advice on the restoration of mental health—and indeed it has already been so to many. There is room here for only a few of his precepts:

> The heights of the spirit can only be ascended by entering at the gate of humility.
>
> If when I meet a man I censure his weakness I deprive myself of the power to attain to higher knowledge; if in a spirit of love I look for what is praiseworthy in him, I am storing up this power.
>
> The knowledge that you seek merely to enhance your knowledge, merely to store up treasures for yourself, will lead

you astray from your road; but the knowledge that you seek in order to ennoble mankind and advance the development of the world will carry you a step forward.

Every idea that does not become to you an ideal destroys an active principle in your mind; but every idea that becomes to you an ideal creates vital forces in you.

So order all your acts and words as not to encroach upon the free will of any man.

Create for yourself moments of inner repose and in these moments learn to distinguish the *essential* from the *non-essential*.

It will always be found that those who possess real knowledge are the most unassuming and that nothing is further from their thoughts than what men call the lust for power.

Even the wisest can learn an infinite amount from children.

If you do not understand something, rather than condemn, do not judge at all.

You must set aside all prejudices.

Without sound common sense every step you take will be in vain.

Learn to be silent about your spiritual visions.

The golden rule is: whenever you attempt to take one step forward in the knowledge of hidden truths, take three steps forward towards the perfection of your character for good.

As a rule, to tread the path of inner growth is given only to those who with energy and perseverance devote themselves to mastering their thoughts and feelings, and the impulses of their will. The resources for such self-control and spiritual activity are derived from meditation, practised in complete stillness. By such concentration and meditation, pursued with inward energy, even a Westerner can attain to knowledge of higher spheres commensurate with the degree of his own development. Rudolf Steiner wrote this book as an aid to the seekers after these matters.

Theologians of both Christian confessions have objected to

the meditative path of spiritual exercises on the grounds that
it is a means to 'self-redemption' that is in contradiction with
the fundamental Christian doctrine of Grace and Redemp-
tion through Jesus Christ. This is a valid objection. All the
instructions that Rudolf Steiner gave to those practising
meditation are about what the human being does and can do.
And Steiner's first concern was that people should not take
life as it comes but develop the highest degree of creative
activity. But what is the scope of this inner activity? In
addition to other faculties that it is intended to develop, it
must restore to the hollow human being of today the capacity
for inner peace, for hearing and listening, for veneration and
devotion. It is in this way that he will encounter the Heavenly
Grace that is as essential to the growth of the soul as the sun
is to plants. The law that applies above all to the domain of
knowledge is that no one acquires higher knowledge who has
not conceived it. And this power to conceive means above all
patience, the ability to wait, expectation. Greed for knowledge harms the striver after knowledge.

> There is a need, without talking a great deal about the concept
> of grace, to do something practical about it.
> There is a need at the present day to suppress the 'greed for
> knowledge'. Rather should we say to ourselves: Grace has
> revealed to me certain truths, and I will wait patiently until
> further truths come to me.
> This is a practical lesson in the exploration of the spiritual
> spheres, particularly in their relation to the phenomenon of
> Christ. It is a radical error in man to suppose that he can
> grasp that which reaches him as it were in a passive way. For
> we must be conscious that we can only be what we are
> intended to be if the spiritual powers judge us so to be. And
> anything we do by way of meditation, contemplation, and so
> on serves only to open our eyes and is not the means
> whereby we grasp those truths which are to be revealed to

us and which we may not pursue (*From Jesus to Christ*, lecture of 8 October 1911).

The human being must play his part to the utmost. Only then can he put his trust in Grace. The words: 'And of his fullness have we all received, and grace for grace' (John 1, 16) are applicable in their fullest sense to Steiner.

An Outline of Esoteric Science

In this third standard work on anthroposophy Rudolf Steiner goes beyond the scope of the first two in that he introduces a general cosmology. This book appeared in 1910 and brings together much of the material which embodies the results of his spiritual research, which he had added to bit by bit over the years in which he was giving study courses. The central themes of *Theosophy*, the nature of the human being, and of *How to Know Higher Worlds*, the schooling path, are here looked at from a new point of view. However he has added the all-important chapter: 'Cosmic Evolution and the Human Being'.

The title *An Outline of Esoteric Science* can quite easily give rise to misunderstandings. Something 'esoteric' is made public; something that has been hidden, esoteric, as far as our senses are concerned, but which is brought to light by the spirit. This is 'revealed knowledge' in the truest sense of the word.

In his preface Steiner comes to grips with all the objections and strictures that can possibly be made about a book of this nature. He finds it quite understandable that scientists should accuse the author of dilettantism, ignorance, and even worse. In answer, Steiner points out that he had himself made a thorough study of science and that he had made it a rule *only to speak or write about those matters in the field of spiritual knowledge where he was able to state, in a manner that seemed satisfactory to himself, what present-day science knows about them.*

Throughout his life he had demonstrated many times that he was entitled to speak in this way. Only one instance will be mentioned here. According to the book, the visible world originated in a spiritual 'thermal element' in which exalted godlike beings (the Seraphim, Cherubim and Thrones of Jewish-Christian terminology) offered sacrifices and did the work of creation. Ten years after the publication of the book Rudolf Steiner gave a course of fourteen lectures on this thermal theory for scientists and teachers in which he demonstrated that he had the facts of thermodynamics right down to their mathematical principles at his fingertips. It would be going too far in this monograph to attempt an account of the contents of *An Outline of Esoteric Science.* The reader who wishes to study them must turn to the book itself. But there is one fact that we cannot ignore. In the *Philosophy of Freedom, Theosophy,* and *How to Know Higher Worlds* you will look in vain for the name of Jesus Christ. Many people have wondered why this should be so. At least as early as 1900 the appearance of Jesus Christ on earth had become for Rudolf Steiner the *central historical event* of the world and of humanity. Witness *Christianity as Mystical Fact.* So why is it that in these works Steiner does not mention Christ and Christianity? Our reply would be: because he was a Christian. 'Thou shalt not take the name of the Lord thy God in vain' was a commandment that Steiner observed in using the name of Jesus Christ. He used this exalted name very sparingly and uttered it only when the circumstances made it necessary. And in relation to *An Outline of Esoteric Science* the circumstances did make it necessary.

CHRISTOLOGY

When John the Evangelist has Jesus Christ say: 'For I know whence I come and whither I go' (John 8, 14), these words by Christ about himself are in accordance with the facts as Rudolf Steiner represents them in his Christology. Christianity as a historical phenomenon, beginning in Bethlehem and continuing through Golgotha to the Church of Christ, on earth has temporal limits. Christ's essence is eternal, that is it has to be thought of as reaching at once backwards into the past and forwards into the future—not otherwise than in the biblical formula: who was (at all times in the past), is (in the present), and ever shall be (forever)—whose kingdom shall know no end. Whereas at the mention of the word and concept 'Eternity' most Christians

Christian Morgenstern
(1871–1914)

cease to think, for Steiner this 'was' and 'shall be' are imbued with life.

Whom, asks Steiner, were the Persians, Egyptians, Greeks, and Germanic tribes looking for when, in their temples and holy places, they worshipped and prayed to the exalted Sun Being under ever new names—Ahura Mazda, Osiris-Horus, Apollo, Balder? Ultimately, no other being than the one who later became man in the body of Jesus of Nazareth. For the exalted Sun Being, whom the pre-Christian religions worshipped, dwelt and was operative in the higher sphere. At the baptism in the river Jordan the God who in ages past was as it were at home in the Sun World beyond the earth, took possession of a man, Jesus of Nazareth, in the three years in which he did his work on earth, until his death on the cross at Golgotha.

It is impossible to understand how all this hangs together unless one sets out from the assumption that the sun is not merely a ball of gas which obeys the material laws of physics and whose energy is dissipated aimlessly and without guidance according to the dictates of chance—somewhat in the manner of a nuclear explosion of hydrogen. Steiner puts the astro-physical view of the sun in a spiritual setting. He draws an analogy between the spiritual man that the physical, corporeal man sees in vision and the Exalted Sun Being of Christ, whose mansion before he came down to earth was the visible sun. The poet Christian Morgenstern found these words to express this aspect of Rudolf Steiner's Christology:

> Seize firmly on the truth revealed,
> Aspiring upwards to the sun,
> And sense the bliss of those above
> By whom creation's work is done
>
> Mount with the spirits to the spheres
> Until the empyrean you gain

And there behold in majesty
The Lord of all the spirits reign

Descend with him to earth again
And there with men and demons live.
Enter with him that reverent man
Who did to him a lodging give

What heart can know his sacrifice?
What spirit measure what he bore?
That God, forsaking Heaven above,
Should live on earth, despised and poor!

(From *Wir fanden einen Pfad*, Munich 1914)

Jesus of Nazareth was a man, Christ the Logos—God. From the baptism in the River Jordan onwards, the God-Man, the Son of Man of the gospels, began to do His work on earth.

The birth of Jesus is the preparation for this divine mission on earth, to which it is mysteriously linked—the gospels speak of it as brought about by the power of the Holy Ghost. Matthew and Luke give conflicting accounts of this super-natural event through which we are enabled to penetrate these mysteries. They give two descriptions of the descent of Jesus, and at first glance it would seem that if one of them is true the other cannot possibly be. But both are right. Rudolf Steiner gives a surprising interpretation of the old theological problem of the 'two Jesus Children'. The first work which he published that contains references to this theme was *The Spiritual Guidance of Man and Humanity* (1911). Privately he had dealt with this theme very fully before this, for instance in the course of lectures at Basle on the Gospel of Luke (1909). According to Steiner everything that the gos-pels relate is to be taken quite literally: 'the earth quaked'—'the sun was darkened'—'the veil of the temple was torn'. But this belief in the literal truth of the gospels is not to be equated to blind faith, but is a challenge to accept the spiritual truth of the physical events.

> At Golgotha, the power, the impulse, that before could flow from the sun to the earth only as light, began to unite itself to the earth; and because the Logos had begun to unite itself to the earth, the earth acquired a new aura.
>
> The physical events of Golgotha are the expression, the revelation, of a spiritual phenomenon that is at the centre of all earthly events. Whoever interprets these words in the light of the materialistic world philosophy of the present day will not be able to make very much of them. For he will not be able to comprehend that these unique happenings at Golgotha are different in kind from similar physical events. There is a vast difference between the earthly events before and after Golgotha.
>
> If the events of Golgotha had never happened, the earth and the sun could never have become united. For Golgotha, whereby the power of the Logos became united to the earth, was the urge that drew the power of the Logos to the power of the Logos and will at the end bring sun and earth together again. Since Golgotha the earth has possessed the spiritual power that will bring it back to union with the sun. We therefore say: the earth's spiritual essence absorbed that which before flowed to it from outside: the power of the Logos— through the events of Golgotha. What was it that had lived on earth before then? The power that flowed from the sun to the earth. What has lived on earth since then? *The Logos itself, which because of Golgotha has become the spirit of the earth.* (Hamburg 1908).

The pre-Christian mystery religions understood these implications, so that the coming of the Messiah, the long awaited Saviour of the world, could be foretold in prophesies. In the mystery schools of the initiates (Osiris-Isis cult, Adonis cult, and others), the symbolic rites of burial and resurrection were enacted as a preparation for the future. At Golgotha, what had before been a rite and a symbol became a historical event: death and resurrection as a physical and spiritual reality.

The raising of Lazarus is to be seen in the same light. A man was raised from the dead in the full glare of publicity ('but because of the people which stand by', John 11, 42), something which would normally have been done only by hierophants in their strictly guarded circle. The guardians of the Mystery Tradition which was also known to and observed by Jewry regarded the resurrection of Lazarus as a betrayal of the Mysteries. ('But the chief priests consulted that they might put Lazarus also to death', John 12, 10). And in all the religions of antiquity the penalty for betrayal of the Mysteries was death. This explains their inexorable determination to destroy Jesus Christ.

The Apostles' Creed, the ancient Christian confession of faith, speaks of Christ's descent into Hell between His death on Good Friday and His resurrection on Easter Morning. 'Descended into Hell'—according to Steiner this describes, not a myth or a legend but an event of a spiritual nature that really occurred, and one that filled with light the darkened souls of those who had died before Christ's time on earth. ('To give light to them that sit in darkness and in the shadow of death', Luke 1, 79).

Then—early on Easter morning—came the resurrection of the body, something which had never happened before on earth and was never to happen again. The supreme power of the spirit of Christ transformed the body, wrested from it the phantom that is an integral part of every human body, and burned the remains to ashes, which the earth swallowed up.

The body that the women and the disciples observed from Easter morning onwards was no physical body. It passed through closed doors ('the doors were shut,' John 20, 19). His was a transformed body, the germ on earth of a new humanity that was to endure for all future time. The primitive Christians sensed this with a kind of clairvoyance.

The primitive Christians drew their strength from the memories of eye-witnesses of Christ's life on earth: 'which we have heard, which we have seen with our own eyes and our hands have handled' (1 John, 1, 1) and from the supernatural experiences of his followers: 'And that he was seen of Cephas, then of the twelve. After that he was seen of above five hundred brethren at once. After that he was seen of James, then of all the apostles. And last of all he was seen of me also' (1 Cor. 15, 5–8).

Thus memory is preserved in the gospels and in church tradition, though in a weakened form, but supersensory perception is dead and gone.

This is the point at which Rudolf Steiner's new teaching of Christ makes its impact. He turns his attention towards Damascus, towards the supernatural experience of Paul, once the fanatical enemy of the Christians, and the vision of John on the island of Patmos, to which we owe the book of Revelation. What these two key witnesses experienced long ago will in a new, modified form become an increasingly frequent phenomenon in the life of modern man, with his acute awareness of his own ego. People will from now on have experiences of Christ which are devoid of any trace of subjectivity. A new faculty for the perception of the ethereal sphere of the resurrected Christ will now be conferred on the human being, so that he will be able to know, in a way that leaves no doubt as to the reality of the experience, the objective and succouring presence of Christ. This will bring about a palpable spiritual change in some members of the human family. The new faculty of perception will be communicated to many, and this in turn will strengthen faith. For Steiner believes that Christianity is for *all* human beings and not for the chosen few. For him it is fatuous to talk about 'knowledge taking the place of faith'. He holds firmly by the words that Jesus Christ spoke to Thomas: 'Blessed are they that have not seen and yet have believed' (John 20, 29). But the new start that will inaugurate a new Christian era on earth will be made when the faculty of supersensory perception that anthroposophy would like to see developed, makes its impact.

> And in time to come, human beings, though only a small company at first, will be privileged to have the same experience as Paul before Damascus and to behold the ethereal Christ, come in supernatural form among us. (Neuchâtel 1911)
>
> The purpose of spiritual science is to enable human beings to understand the new powers that will be seen in action among them...
>
> Christ will return, but in a form that transcends physical reality, a form that only he can look upon who has come to understand spiritual life...
>
> Engrave in your hearts what anthroposophy is to be; a preparation for the great human epoch that lies ahead of us. (Berlin 1910)
>
> No one can understand the events of Golgotha who does not understand them in a spiritual sense. Thus the spiritual science of anthroposophy is at the same time an initiation into a new understanding of Christ and the Mystery of Golgotha. (Prague 1923)

ANTHROPOSOPHY IN ART

The Mystery Dramas

Rudolf Steiner's lecture on 'The Nature of the Arts', which he gave in Berlin on 28 October 1909, is like the overture to a new act of his working life. For this lecture is not a talk 'on art' by an expert, but is from first to last a consciously created work of art.

But the first presages of this new development in Steiner's life belong to an earlier date. At the fourth annual congress of the Federation of European Branches of the Theosophical Society at Munich in 1907, the first dramatic productions were staged.

> Artistic productions were included in the programme for the congress. A long time earlier, Marie von Sivers had translated Schuré's reconstruction of the Eleusinian drama. I edited the text for a theatrical presentation and we added this drama to the programme. This provided a link with the ancient mysteries, albeit a rather tenuous one—but the real point about it was that the congress now had an artistic side. An indication of the intention henceforth not to conduct the spiritual life of the Society without some attention to the claims of art.

Munich seemed predestined to be the seat for the manifestations of this aspect of anthroposophy. The atmosphere here was one in which the artistic element could thrive.

'Berlin and Munich represented as it were the two opposite poles of anthroposophical activity.' Berlin was steeped in rationalism and intellectualism. Here anthroposophy would develop as an exercise in lucid thinking.

In Munich it was otherwise. There, right from the start the artistic element had become interwoven with the anthroposophical work. Art's way of absorbing a philosophy like anthroposophy was quite different from that of rationalism and intellectualism. Artistic representation is fuller of spirituality than the rationalistic concept. Moreover, it is alive and does not destroy what is spiritual in the mind, as intellectualism does. In Munich, the personalities who took the lead in creating a membership and an audience were those in whom art awakened susceptibilities of this kind.

And so it happened that in Berlin the Society developed from the start as one branch at unity with itself. The interests of the seekers after anthroposophy were identical. In Munich, artistic invention created divers needs in divers circles, and it was to these circles that I lectured.

It is obvious that this artistic work in Munich, which regularly until 1913 reached its climax in August, brought

Edouard Schuré
(1841–1929)

A list of the dramatic works presented in Munich under the direction of Rudolf Steiner. (In Rudolf Steiner Selbsterkenntnis, *Nachlassverwaltung, Dornach 1950)*

1907

19th May:	Original production of *The Sacred Drama of Eleusis* by E. Schuré

1909

22nd August:	Original production of *The Children of Lucifer* by E. Schuré

1910

14th August:	First revival of *The Children of Lucifer* by E. Schuré
15th August:	Original production of *The Portal of Initiation* by R. Steiner

1911

13th August:	First revival of *The Sacred Drama of Eleusis* by E. Schuré
15th August:	First revival of *The Portal of Initiation* by R. Steiner
17th August:	Original production of *The Soul's Probation* by R. Steiner

1912

18th August:	Second revival of *The Sacred Drama of Eleusis* by E. Schuré
20th August:	Second revival of *The Portal of Initiation* by R. Steiner
22nd August:	First revival of *The Soul's Probation* by R. Steiner
24th August:	Original production of *The Guardian of the Threshold* by R. Steiner

1913

19th August:	First revival of *The Guardian of the Threshold* by R. Steiner
20th August:	Second revival of *The Guardian of the Threshold* by R. Steiner
22th August:	Original production of *The Souls' Awakening* by R. Steiner
23rd August:	First revival of *The Souls' Awakening* by R. Steiner
28th August:	The first Eurythmy display.

The outbreak of war in August 1914 put an end to plans for further productions.

about many contacts with artists living in Munich who had no links with anthroposophy. Among the audiences at the lectures were men like Vasily Kandinsky and Alexei von Jawlensky, who came to Steiner for advice on personal matters without thereby establishing any relationship with anthroposophy.

We learn from the Kandinsky monograph by Will Grohmann (Dumont Schauberg Verlag) that Kandinsky painted the Ariel scene, in 1908, after attending a lecture by Steiner. 'Perhaps there can be seen here some influence of the spiritual insight of Rudolf Steiner, whom he had come into contact with in Berlin ... Kandinsky was at one with Steiner in feeling that a catastrophe was impending, that science had failed and that there was a need for spiritual insight.'

After the original production of Edouard Schuré's *The Children of Lucifer* in 1909, from 1910 onwards Rudolf Steiner's Mystery Dramas became an integral part of the anthroposophical work. The first of his mystery dramas was presented in 1910. This was followed by a new one every year until 1913.

1910 *The Portal of Initiation*
1911 *The Soul's Probation*
1912 *The Guardian of the Threshold*
1913 *The Souls' Awakening*

A fifth drama was planned for 1914, but was never presented owing to the war.

These dramas were acted by professionals and amateurs with the utmost dedication. Eyewitnesses tell us that they made a profound impression on the audiences, who were mostly members of the Theosophical, later the Anthroposophical, Society, who were well prepared to receive their message.

We are doing a disservice to these dramas if we compare them with traditional drama. They are to be understood as 'mystery dramas'. Human destinies, linked by successive lives on earth, are traced. We are shown the pilgrims of the spirit who have travelled the road of self-knowledge and have been guided to the threshold of the spiritual world, each in his own way. In the life of meditation they meet trials and find consolation which go beyond the bounds of normal earthly experience. Things experienced in the present become windows on to the Middle Ages, and through them to Ancient Egypt.

Dramatic tension in the conventional sense there is none. Stage effects are deliberately eschewed. One might call these mystery dramas Rudolf Steiner's revelations of the spirit as an art form—embodying as they do almost all the knowledge to be found in Steiner's books about man and his destiny through successive lives on earth, presented in dramatic form.

The first Goetheanum under construction (February 1914)

His collaborators recall that Steiner wrote each play in successive stages a day at a time, bringing what he had written the previous night with him each morning. While it was he who directed the whole production, from the instructions about the costumes and the stage settings to the actual stage management, it was Marie von Sivers, later to become Marie Steiner, who was the moving spirit behind it all. Her earlier career had been a preparation for this task. She had received training in St Petersburg from eminent actors, and had continued her training in Paris. She had been just about to embark on a stage career when anthroposophy came into her ken, whereupon she gave up all thought of an acting career. She was endowed by nature with a remarkable voice. Recitation was her forte. And so she stood at Rudolf Steiner's right hand and helped to stage his plays.

On 24 August 1913, Christian Morgenstern wrote from

The first Goetheanum, view from the south

Munich to his friend, the actor Friedrich Kayssler, describing his impressions of the mystery drama:

'Steiner's Mystery is not a play but a portrayal of spiritual spheres and truths. It ushers in a new stage of achievement, a new artistic age—although its production was beset with many of the difficulties that arise when something new is attempted. This age lies still in the future; centuries may pass before those who need this purely spiritual art become so numerous that in virtually every city such mystery drama can be presented and received in a manner that befits it. But here in the "Portal" is its historical origin, here we are present at its birth. Something tremendous is unfolded before our eyes—mountain vastnesses of the spirit, which a lifetime would not suffice to search out and know thoroughly.'

The productions were staged in many different theatres in

The auditorium during construction

Munich, in the Schauspielhaus, in the Theater am Gärtner-
platz, and in the Volkstheater. The stages of these theatres
were satisfactory enough in the ordinary sense of the word,
but as settings for these mystery dramas with their appeal to
the spirit they could not have been more unsuitable. There
was a need for a building in which these productions could be
housed in an atmosphere that was in harmony with their
spiritual nature. The Johannes-Bau-Verein was established
with the aim of erecting in Munich a building that should
provide both a stage for the presentation of the mystery
dramas and a centre for anthroposophical activity in Germany. This plan came to grief after several false starts. In its
place, friends in Switzerland offered a site at Dornach near
Basle with ample space for the erection of a building. Rudolf
Steiner went there, inspected the site, and accepted the offer.

The First Goetheanum

A gift of fate! The year was 1913. One year later the First
World War broke out. Switzerland, at the very heart of
Europe, was spared from all disasters—as it was also in the
Second World War. And thus Rudolf Steiner was enabled to
erect the first Goetheanum in the triangle where France,
Germany, and Switzerland meet. The choice of name for this
building was a further reminder to the world at large of how
ardently Rudolf Steiner wished his anthroposophy to be
linked to Goethe's essential nature and his work.

The foundation stone was laid in 1913 and the foundation
ceremony took place in 1914. Within earshot of the gunfire
from the Vosges, which were visible from the hill of Dornach,
devotees from seventeen different countries worked together
to produce art forms for this, the first centre for the anthroposophical movement. A wooden building with two domes,
in an entirely new style, was erected on a concrete foun-

Rudolf Steiner in the studio (1919)

dation. In order to erect the double dome over a stage and an auditorium for about 1000 persons, unusual mathematical and engineering problems had to be solved. The construction costs, amounting to more than seven million Swiss francs, were met by donations.

Architects, workers in the sculptural arts, and painters worked together at the same task and—always under the direction and with the practical assistance of Rudolf Steiner—laid the foundations of the anthroposophical architecture, sculpture, and painting that remains controversial to this day.

Many architectural plans and sketches for paintings from Steiner's own hand survive from this period. Caricatures which he dashed off at odd times on paper napkins over tea reveal glimpses of his humour.

A figure of Christ was to have been erected at the rear of the stage in the eastern part of the building. The 'Representative of Humanity' stood erect between the two adver-

Haus de Jaager

saries, Lucifer the hypocritical tempter and Ahriman the grim destroyer. Rudolf Steiner created this sculpture mainly himself, with hammer and chisel—but unfortunately his early death prevented him from completing it. It was saved from the fire that destroyed the Goetheanum in 1923 and is today one of the most important works from Steiner's own hand.

Eurythmy

Architecture, the sculptural arts, and painting have been a part of all civilizations. Art always reflects the spirit of the age. The pyramids of Egypt, the Greek temples, the medieval cathedrals, are each a manifestation of their age. In giving a new stimulus to these arts, Steiner was acting in character with the civilizing urge of anthroposophy. Particularly in the Berlin and Munich periods, artists of standing frequently turned to him for advice. But eurythmy is something new. It is neither gymnastics nor dancing—nor is it mime. True, it is an art of motion, but at the same time it is an 'art of consciousness'. To understand this we have to strip from the word 'consciousness' everything that is suggestive of 'intellectuality'. No art comes from the intellect, which is the enemy of all true art. The aim of eurythmy is to make visible by gesture and movement the *spiritual* conformity and quality of words and sounds, and make of them an artistic experience. This requires 'spiritual consciousness', which makes the unseen vital processes that lie behind every uttered vowel or consonant, every syllable, every word, every sound, something that can be enjoyed as an artistic experience. From this subjective-objective experience eurythmy is born as *visible speech*, as *visible song*. Starting in a very modest way in 1912, eurythmy under the aegis of Marie Steiner developed in three directions: as stage art, as an educational aid in schools, and as a therapeutic method.

In the very last year of his life Rudolf Steiner conducted two eurythmy courses comprising in all 23 lectures, giving a complete exposition of his views on this new art form. The Dornach school in Switzerland and many other schools elsewhere have since demonstrated on many European stages to what extent the stimulus he gave has been developed into real achievement. Since modern dancing has developed under the influence of the rhythms of Africa and America, which appeal solely to the sub-conscious and the unconscious, it seems as if eurythmy will have a kind of therapeutic effect on human movement. Here are some aphorisms of Steiner about eurythmy:

> Man as we see him before us is complete in himself. But this completeness is the result of motion ... And when we develop eurythmy we are carried back to the very beginnings of motion ... God does eurythmy, and in so doing produces the human form.
>
> ... for eurythmy means in a certain sense the making of gestures, yet not transient random gestures, but cosmic ones, loaded with meaning, such as cannot be otherwise and are not due to any human caprice. (*Eurythmy as Visible Speech*, lecture of 24 June 1924.)
>
> There is perhaps no art in which one is made so intensely aware of being at one with the cosmos, as in eurythmy.

Marie Steiner: 'Eurythmy means: Singing as movement. It is song. It is not dance, it is not mime; it is singing.'

Speech Formation

To understand the relationship in which Steiner stood to language, one had to hear him speak. The natural intonation of his warm voice was full of the cordiality of the Viennese idiom. It was naturally endowed with an astounding range, so that he was able for instance to take all the parts in the mystery dramas himself. While in the ordinary course of events he gave pride of place to Marie Steiner, as the trained speaker, nevertheless he frequently gave amazing proofs of his abilities as a speaker. The last time this happened was in September 1924, at the end of his public life, during a course which he gave on 'Speech Formation and Dramatic Art'. In this course for speakers and actors he was aiming at something which was implicit from the start in his activities prior to the anthroposophical period, something which led him to call the Goetheanum the *House of Language and the House of the Word.*

In his *Autobiography* he quotes what he wrote in the *Dramaturgische Blätter* of March 1898 about elocution.

> It is rarely that everyday speech becomes raised to the level of an art. We are almost entirely bereft of feeling for the beauty of speech, still more bereft of feeling for speech that is in character ... People nowadays often consider artistic speaking

Marie Steiner, née von Sivers (1867–1948), in 1915

to be misguided idealism. This would never have happened if people had been more aware of the possibility of developing speech as an art

and he continues (1925):

What I then envisaged did not find fulfilment until very much later, in the Anthroposophical Society. Marie von Sivers (Marie Steiner), who was an enthusiast on the subject of elocution, made a study of purely artistic speaking, and with her help speech formation and drama courses were started with the aim of raising these accomplishments to the level of true art.

At Dornach the Speech School was founded as a part of the Section for Spoken Arts and Music. Here professional speakers, actors and teachers have been trained for decades past.

LECTURING ACTIVITIES—THE FIRST WORLD WAR

With each passing year the scale of Rudolf Steiner's lecturing activities increased. Individual lectures to the public or to an intimate circle of students of anthroposophy alternated with the lecture series, which in some cities were spread over two weeks. Everything published in his books can also be found in these lectures. But there is much in these lectures which is not to be found in his works. The members of the Anthroposophical Society therefore felt the need to have the lecture series printed. Steiner consented to this only with reluctance, since he was strongly aware of the difference between the spoken and the written word. But he gave way. The majority of the 6000 lectures that he gave have now been printed, and the literary executors have published a complete edition which includes them along with his books, essays, etc.

Steiner had already in earlier years made foreign lecture tours—for instance in 1906 he gave 18 lectures in Paris, Edouard Schuré and Merezhkovski being among his audiences—but 1908, with one visit to the Netherlands and two to Scandinavia, marked the start of the intensification of his Europe-wide activities, which continued to expand right up to the outbreak of the First World War.

Shortly before the outbreak of war, having been lecturing at Norrköping in Sweden, he was at Bayreuth for the Festival performances (Parsifal) at the end of July. During the war he lived alternately in Dornach and Berlin. At the end of August the chief of the German General Staff, Generaloberst Helmuth von Moltke, asked him to come to Coblenz to discuss certain matters with him. Ill-wishers made the most grotesque accusations about the subject of these discussions. The loss of the Battle of the Marne, and with it the defeat of Germany, was actually ascribed to his 'magical influence'. Von Moltke had come to have confidence in Steiner and sought his advice on private matters. The discussions had nothing whatever to do with the military situation.

On 24 December 1914 Steiner married Marie von Sivers. Anna Steiner, whose former married name had been Eunike, had died in 1911.

In certain French quarters, and even for a time by Edouard Schuré, Steiner was charged with too much partiality to Germany during the war. Careful study of what Steiner had to say, particularly in 1914 to 1916, certainly shows that he set his face against the policy of extermination promulgated by the Entente powers and had hard words to say about it. But at no time is his position that of a German chauvinist. At Oslo in 1910 he had spoken at great length about the mission of individual nations and argued that each had a part to play in the community of nations that matched its individual mental characteristics.* In this connection, Steiner had a deeply rooted faith in the spiritual mission of the German people. Of Wilhelm II and his vain lust for power he thought nothing, it is true. But he thought all the more of the people that had produced Goethe, Schiller, Fichte, Schelling, Hegel. He did not look on this mission as ended and still hoped for great things from it.

Wilson's peace programme with its appeal to the egoism of races and nations he rejected as an illusion. He foresaw that the right of self-determination for the tiniest national fragments—sucessful though it has been in the case of Switzerland with its three national languages—would not provide

---

* *The Mission of the Individual Folk Souls in Relation to Teutonic Mythology.*

Rudolf Steiner, 1920

real solutions for social problems and genuine problems of state. Steiner's efforts to avert the German tragedy through discussions with leading politicians (for instance with the foreign minister, Richard von Kühlmann, before the negotiations at Brest-Litovsk) and memoranda (to the Emperor Charles of Austria through the Secretary to his Cabinet, Arthur Graf Polzer-Hoditz), availed nothing to prevent the German tragedy.

After the collapse in 1919 Rudolf Steiner made an appeal: *To the German People and the Civilized World.*

> The German People was secure in its belief that the Empire it had founded half a century ago would endure for countless years to come. In August 1914 it believed that the catastrophic war with which it was then faced would prove this empire to be an impregnable stronghold. Today it sees it in ruins. After passing through such an experience it is time to reflect. For this experience has shown up the opinion of the past half-century,

has exposed the thinking of the war years as an error with
tragic consequences. What is at the root of this error? This is a
question which must give the German people pause for
thought. The future of the German people depends on whether it possesses the capacity for reflection, and on whether it
can give a meaningful answer to the question; how did I fall
into this error? If it asks itself this question today it will realize
that half a century ago it founded an empire but neglected to
assign to it a task relevant to the essential nature of the German people.

Then follows a firm injunction to break up the hitherto
compact structure of the state into its three constituent
elements: the spiritual, the political, and the economic. Only
by unravelling the social structure and differentiating
between its three constituent elements will it be possible to
avoid the impending chaos. The appeal ends:

> Either we consent to respect in our thinking the claims of
> reality, or, having learned nothing from misfortune, we com-
> pound the events of the past to infinity by the events yet to
> come.

Of the persons who signed this appeal, many have never
associated themselves with anthroposophy or did so subsequently. But they were prepared to contribute to the realization of the ideas advanced in this appeal and to set their
names to it. Among the signatures we find those of: Prof. Dr.
Hans Driesch, Heidelberg; Prof. Dr. Hans Ehrenberg, Heidelberg; Prof. Dr. R. Gaupp, Tübingen; Prof. Dr. Goldstein,
Frankfurt; Prof. Hugo von Habermann, Munich; Hermann
Hesse, author, Berne; W. J. Hilger, director of Hansa-Lloyd-
Werke, Bremen; Theodor Kappstein, author, Charlotten-
burg; Prof. Kärcher, Karlsruhe; Prof. Dr. Kippenberg,
Bremen; Prof. Dr. Theodor Landau, Charlottenberg; Wil-
helm Lehmbruck, sculptor, Zürich; Le Seur, minister of

religion, Berlin-Lichterfelde; Prof. Dr. Friedrich Lienhard, author, Weimar; Prof. Dr. Paul Natorp, privy councillor, Marburg; Prof. Dr. Ludwig Oehninger, Berlin; Dr. Alfons Paquet, author, Frankfurt; Max von Pauer, director of the Conservatory, Stuttgart; Dr. von Pechmann, director of the Handelsbank, Munich; Martin Rade, doctor of theology, Marburg; Gabriele Reuter, authoress, Berlin; Prof. Dr. Schauinsland, director of the Ethnological Museum, Bremen; E. Schlegel, Tübingen; Dr. Wilhelm von Scholz, author and dramatist, Stuttgart; Siegmund-Schultze, director of the civic Youth Department, Berlin; Richard Seebohm, Major, retired, Kassel; Traugott von Stackelberg, Munich; Dr. Hans Hasso von Veltheim, director, Munich; Dr. H. Voith, manufacturer, Heidenheim; Prof. Dr. Kurt Wolzendorff, Königsberg; Dr. Hugo Sinzheimer, member of the National Assembly, Frankfurt; Prof. Dr. Otto, Frankfurt.

The movement which Rudolf Steiner created, with the aim of solving the problem of society, and which came to be known as the Threefold Social Order, was the direct outcome of this appeal.

THE THREEFOLD SOCIAL ORDER
(1918–1921)

While the roots of theosophy are the insights it affords into the spiritual world, these are still only its roots. Its branches, leaves, blossom, and fruits are to be found growing in every field of human life and endeavour.

The period of Rudolf Steiner's life in which these words were to be substantiated openly began with the tragic conclusion of the First World War. Since 1916 he had contemplated the possibility of the defeat of the central powers. Behind it he was aware of the gigantic presence of the social problem. Implicit in his teaching activities in the years 1916–1918 was his concern to awaken in people, primarily in the members of the Anthroposophical Society, understanding of this enigma of the twentieth century.

On 9 November, the day of the revolution in Germany, he started a lecture series in Dornach on 'Historical Grounds for the Formulation of a Social Judgement'. In Central Europe, depression and despair were abroad. Steiner for his part sought to counter this mood with wholesome thoughts. Wherever the opportunity arose he spoke about the 'nub of the social problem', and wherever possible he tried to give practical help with social problems. There were many such opportunities. For a time at least the workers of Württemberg were in a receptive mood. Steiner received appeals for help from many quarters. In Stuttgart in April he spoke to a meeting of thousands of Bosch, Delmonte, and Daimler workers. This was no kid-glove affair. Steiner stood up well to the tough atmosphere of the meetings of works councils and workers' committees. Many people came to trust in him. The 'Association for the Threefold Organization of Society' was founded with the object of putting his social ideas into practice. It was joined by many people who were otherwise quite unconnected with anthroposophy.

The fundamental idea behind this Threefold Social Order was that social life can only prosper if it is consciously organized. The individual who has come to rely on himself can no longer acknowledge the supreme power of the State. The capacity of the individual for work must not be degraded to the level of a commodity. The State and Industry must be so organized as not to impair the dignity of the worker.

It is Steiner's view that in order to achieve these aims it is necessary to sever the ties between the state, industry, and the life of the spirit.

1. The state that we have known hitherto (and most particularly all the totalitarian states that have come into being since 1919, and some of which have had their day!) have overstepped, and continue to overstep, the limits assigned to

Rudolf Steiner, 1915

them. The role of the constitutional state should be limited to actual political life, and its task should be limited to the protection of its citizens from internal and external dangers. The poor laws, the labour code, and criminal law, with the means for enforcing it (the police, the army) should come under the sway of the state. But nothing further! Under the state there should be *equality* for all.

2. But the state should not itself carry on industrial enterprises. More and more, industry is extending its range. Many nations are involved in it, and ultimately all will be involved. The involvement of the state in industrial enterprises should be the exception, not the rule. All the more reason why all those concerned in the industrial process (production, distribution, and consumption) should work together by forming associations of producers and consumers. This means the realization of the ideal of *fraternity*, without any sentimental connotations.

3. And finally: The state should refrain from acting as its citizens' intellectual mentor (the United States are far ahead of Europe in this respect). The *freedom* of art, science (including schools), and religion must be guaranteed.

Intellectual *freedom, equality* before the law, *fraternity* in industry—Rudolf Steiner gave the old ideals of the French Revolution a new realism.

For him, this idea of the tripartite organization of society never became an ideology, to be imposed on the world as a programme, if necessary by force.

It is the facts themselves that dictate that the three elements of the social organization shall be made independent of each other. This, whether or not one recognizes the facts, is for Steiner a question of consciousness.

Have not the years that followed proved him in a very large measure right?

But in 1919 Rudolf Steiner did not achieve what he had set

out to do. Very soon the threefold movement, which had gained a number of very active protagonists, was caught between the upper and lower millstones of the selfishness of the entrepreneurs and the mistrust of the trade union officials. Something which depended on freely formed opinion and good will was made a bone of contention by politicians who wanted no truck with anything genuinely new. As it were overnight, Steiner called off his collaborators and terminated what we regard as this historical endeavour to solve the social problem. The time was not yet ripe. But if social experiments fail at the first attempt, does this mean that they have been in vain? Is the foundering of the first attempt to be judged as embodying the final truth about an idea? Hardly!

THE STEINER WALDORF
EDUCATIONAL MOVEMENT (1919–1924)

The educational movement that Rudolf Steiner inaugurated became known as the Waldorf School Movement. The name is derived from a cigarette factory. As he generally did throughout his life, Rudolf Steiner waited for some external stimulus before deciding to act. In the case of this educational movement, the stimulus came from Emil Molt, the director of the Waldorf-Astoria cigarette factory. This gentleman showed an exceptional degree of concern for the human dignity and the promotion of the interests of the workers and employees of the works of which he was in charge. Workers' educational courses were included in the benefits provided by the firm as a matter of course, in the same way as a works magazine of a high standard, the care of the workers' children, and so on—voluntary social services that were still the exception in those days. The adults themselves expressed the wish that not only they should benefit from this educational work, but also their children. Emil Molt responded to this suggestion, and referred the problems involved to Steiner, asking for his assistance in founding a works school. Thus, one year after the total collapse of the German Empire, in 1919, the first Waldorf School came into being—initially as the works school of a cigarette factory—but in reality the first foundation of an educational movement that was to bear abundant fruit and spread throughout the world.

In his school and student days Steiner had ample opportunity to acquire teaching experience. After all, he had had to earn his pocket money, and later a considerable part of his livelihood, by giving coaching and private lessons to younger students. At the Workers' Educational Institute in Berlin he had taught adults regularly for more than five years. In 1907 he had published a small work: *The Education of the Child.*

Twelve years later he was given the opportunity to turn his thoughts and ideas into deeds. A kind star must have watched over the desperately difficult birth of the anthroposophical educational movement, in that period of ruin for Germany. For looking back, one is astonished at the abundance of teachers of more than average attainments who flocked together within such a short time to form the original teaching staff. People like Stockmeyer, Dr Kolisko, Dr Stein, Professor von Baravalle, Dr Hahn, Dr Lehrs, Dr Schwebsch, Engineer Alexander Strakosch, Ernst Bindel, Ernst Uehli, Maria Röschl, Caroline von Heydebrand, the painter Max Wolfhügel, the musician Paul Baumann, and many more, most of whom later distinguished themselves by publishing works, created the unique, spiritually uplifted atmosphere of the first Waldorf School.

Dr. h.c. Emil Molt
(1876–1936)

The work on education referred to above contains this sentence:

> *If called upon to develop a system of education*, spiritual science will be able to impart everything that comes under this heading, even down to instructions about diet appropriate for children. For it is realistic in its approach to life, not vague theory, although perhaps owing to the aberrations of many theosophists it is made to appear so.

So, now anthroposophy was being called upon to develop such a system of education! This school was dear to Rudolf Steiner's heart. Between 1919 and 1924 he gave no fewer than 15 courses of lectures for teachers and educators in Germany, Britain, and the Netherlands. In these lectures he based the principles of education on the knowledge of the human species that he derived from anthroposophy.

At the end of August 1922 Rudolf Steiner was invited to attend the British Educational Conference at Oxford, the subject of which was: Spiritual Values in Education and Social Life. In England he met with something that he seldom encountered elsewhere: publicly expressed gratitude and recognition.

In the report in the *Manchester Guardian* on 3 August 1922 we read: 'At the centre of the entire Conference stands the personality and doctrine of Dr Rudolf Steiner.

'His lectures, for which we owe him our special thanks, vividly describe a humane educational ideal. He has told us of teachers who freely and in a common effort, unrestricted by regulations and regimentation from outside, have developed their educational methods solely on the basis of their intimate knowledge of human nature. He told us of a kind of knowledge that a teacher needs to have, knowledge of human nature and the world, knowledge that is not only scientific but penetrates to the most intimate inward parts, that is both intuitive and artistic.'

Here, very succinctly, are the main ideas underlying Steiner's plans for education:

The Waldorf School—and all the Steiner Waldorf schools subsequently founded have been based on the same model—is a combined elementary and secondary school divided into twelve classes (today, many Steiner Waldorf schools have an additional 13th class for preparing students for final exams). It is *not* the aim of the school to inculcate a philosophy of the world or teach anthroposophy. A teacher who did so would not be a good Steiner Waldorf teacher. But the educator and teacher proceeds from his own work and life with anthroposophy and the image of man that it projects. The school is concerned solely with general instruction. The young receive the help that they need in order to discover their identity, and later to associate themselves fully with the occupational and cultural life of today's world. From the start the principle of co-education was accepted as a matter of course, boys and girls being taught in the same classes and helping each other, 'consciously—unconsciously', through the polarity of their natures. In these schools, no one lives in fear of not being moved up into the next class—but neither is there the preferential selection of the more gifted pupils which is so often extolled today. Instead, social behaviour is inculcated. Advanced pupils are urged to help the less gifted. In this way they learn to make use of their social aptitudes, which would otherwise lie dormant.

To avoid fragmentation of the curriculum, which produces a fragmented mind, the main instruction is given in daily two-hour periods, continued without interruption for several weeks. Then the main subject changes. These 'period studies' are accompanied by subjects which require constant practice: foreign languages, music and handicrafts, physical education, eurythmy.

From the first to the eighth year the children have the same form teacher, who is responsible for the main part of the teaching. In this way the teacher through years of experience acquires a subtle understanding of his young charges as they grow up. The class becomes a tightly knit community.

From the 9th to the 12th school year the main lessons are given by subject specialists. At this stage the children are frequently directed into a scientific or a practical stream, according to their aptitudes.

Foreign languages are taught right from the first class onwards, in order to introduce the children to them through the medium of natural imitation, by ear, in the same way as they learned their mother tongue. The rules of grammar are not taught until later. Particular importance is attached to the speech of every child, the way in which it frames words. What is aimed at is an intimate relationship to the language.

All teaching should be artistically presented from the 1st to the 8th school year. Manual skills are highly esteemed. Handwork, such as knitting, weaving, plaiting, bookbinding, is a compulsory subject for boys and girls.

The first Waldorf School, Stuttgart, 1919

Michael Hall School, Forest Row, Sussex. Kindergarten in foreground

The curriculum includes carving, woodwork, working with clay, stone, and metal. Painting, and later drawing, are much practised.

The children receive instruction in music, and as a rule learn to play the recorder. Every school has its choir and orchestra. Eurythmy is an essential part of the life of the school.

Gymnastics, sport, and light athletics are of course essential in this present age.

In some countries religious instruction is given by representatives of the various churches in accordance with the wishes of the parents. Children not receiving church instruction are given broad instruction in the Christian religion.

The importance of a relation of real trust between teachers and parents is stressed. Parents' evenings are a regular institution.

The midsummer and advent festivals, the presentation of the Oberufer Christmas plays, and regular celebrations throw a protective mantle over the school, under which parents, teachers, and pupils live as a school community.

The Waldorf School at Stuttgart, 1961

Naturally, these schools have had to face individual crises in the past, and are constantly facing new ones. The main cause of concern is the shortage of subject specialists at the higher level, consequent upon the rapid growth and expansion of the schools. To give up all claim to recognition by an external authority, selfless teachers with strong personalities are needed. The minds of the young must have a high capacity to absorb material if they are to acquire the knowledge that is necessary for a career in the twenty-first century. At the same time they need to be protected against the harmful influences of a materialistic age. At Rudolf Steiner's death in 1925 there were two schools in Germany and one each in the Netherlands and Great Britain.

To date (2000) there are 162 schools in Germany and 642 elsewhere.

MEDICINE (1920–1924)

Soon after the founding of the Waldorf School, Rudolf Steiner was asked whether there was any contribution he could make to the art of healing. What prompted this plea was the crisis in medicine which has since come out into the open. It was all the more germane in that the members of the Anthroposophical Society were aware that as early as 1911 Rudolf Steiner had delivered a series of lectures in Prague on *Occult Physiology*.

From the very first Steiner took steps to guard against the risk that the growing interest in medical matters might lead to the spread of dilettantism among the laity. With a few carefully chosen exceptions he admitted only doctors and medical

The Clinical and Therapeutic Institute at Arlesheim

students to the courses on therapeutics that he conducted in 1920–1924. Here too his knowledge of humanity, gathered through almost two decades in his capacity as teacher of anthroposophy, was fundamental to his teaching.

In his book *Von Seelenrätseln** (1917) he traced the relation between the functioning of the mind and physical processes. This was now applied to physiology. According to the account that he now gives, the dynamics of the healthy human organism are seen as the result of the interaction of three more or less autonomous systems of organs:

1. The nervous and sensory system, the primary conveyor of sensory perceptions and of mental images.
2. The metabolism, of which sexuality and the control of the limbs must be counted parts. It is the physiological seat of the will.
3. The circulatory and respiratory systems (circulation, heart, lungs) which hold the balance between these two polar processes, being the primary means by which feeling is communicated.

Over-activity or break-down of any one of these systems leads to illness.

'Physical Man' and his organs and processes do not make sense, unless at the same time they are considered as expressing something of the 'Supernatural Man'. General chatter about mind and spirit gets nowhere, but this is not true of differentiated knowledge of the parts played by specific organs and systems of organs in the life of the mind and the spirit. In support of these general expressions of opinion Steiner supplies an abundance of indications and data. He indicated to the doctors who questioned him the possibility of the anthroposophical diagnosis of symptoms and instructions for the application of suitable therapeutic

---

* Partially translated in *The Case for Anthroposophy*.

methods. The book entitled *Extending Practical Medicine, Fundamental Principles based on the Science of the Spirit*, which he wrote in collaboration with Ita Wegman MD, the first director of the Medical Section of the Goetheanum and founder of the Arlesheim Clinic, was not published until 1925, after his death. 'There is no question of opposing the scientific methods of modern medicine. We accept without reservation the principles on which these methods are based. And it is our belief that what we have to offer should be used only by those who are fully qualified doctors in the sense of those principles.'

'All that we are doing is to *add* to what it is possible to know about the human being by the application of the currently recognized scientific methods, knowledge found by other methods. Our broadened knowledge of the world and man thus places us in a situation in which we feel bound to work for the extension of medical science.'

Ita Wegman MD
(1876–1943)

The stimulus provided by this book and the lecture courses has brought it about that today, seventy-five years after the death of Rudolf Steiner, more than 2,700 doctors are practising anthroposophic medicine, with many clinics and sanatoria at their service.

The Arlesheim Clinic became the mother foundation of this medical movement. The Medical Section of the Goetheanum was also re-formed some years ago. In Germany, at Easter every year some 200 doctors meet for a conference at Comburg (Schwäbisch Hall). For the so-called 'mentally ill' the psychiatrist Friedrich Husemann MD (died 1959) established the Wiesneck sanatorium at Buchenbach, near Freiburg im Breisgau, with an enclosed section.

The medical courses contained many suggestions about new applications for medicines. It is mainly due to the initiative of the pharmacist Dr Schmiedel that these suggestions led to the establishment of factories for pharmaceutical

Weleda AG., Schwäbisch Gmünd

products at Arlesheim and Schwäbisch Gmünd (Weleda-AG). Resulting from the establishment of these two factories there are today many international branches.

The 'Wala' factory producing medicines and tonics at Stuttgart under the direction of Dr Hauschka came into being in response to the same suggestions.

The Cancer Research Association at Arlesheim, Switzerland, carries out a special programme of medical research. 'The aim of the Association for Cancer Research is to develop a cure for cancer indicated by Rudolf Steiner and to perfect the methods of treatment. This medicament has been given the name "Iscador". It is prepared from a number of species of mistletoe (*Viscum album*) ... The Association is directed by doctors, who, as all doctors, have had daily to contend with cancer in their practices.'

Rudolf Steiner never played the part of a 'healer'. But many people owe their recovery to him and his work. Everyone who knew him intimately in the final period of his life was amazed at his detailed knowledge of medicine. 'Before making pronouncements on spiritual matters, anthroposophy develops the methods that give it the right to make such pronouncements.'

EDUCATION FOR SPECIAL NEEDS (1924)

The increase in the number of special needs children in our day is an undeniable and extremely disturbing fact. Rudolf Steiner started the movement for therapeutic education.

Once again the stimulus came from outside. Three young students had been given the task of caring for such children. They asked Rudolf Steiner for advice, and they did not ask in vain. In 1924 they founded at Jena the first Institute for Therapeutic Education, 'Lauenstein'. Shortly afterwards, children in need of special care began to be received at the Arlesheim Clinic. The 'Sonnenhof' was founded at Arlesheim under the direction of Ita Wegman MD. Who could have foreseen at that time that these two cells, working under the most primitive conditions, could have given rise to a movement which today maintains about 550 establishments in which thousands of children are cared for?

Helgeseter near Bergen (Norway)

The fundamental idea underlying this work, which entails the utmost self-sacrifice, derives directly, and as a matter of course, from anthroposophy. Fate (karma) has placed the minds of these children in sick, misshapen bodies. It has not done this without purpose and in vain. This is a means of communicating experiences which the eternal individuality works on after death and which are matured and given renewed force for a next incarnation. It therefore behoves us to lavish understanding and love on sick children. In a course at Dornach in 1924 Steiner gave the first class of future educational therapists a detailed account of the diseases of children and appealed to them to volunteer for the dedicated profession of educational therapist: 'Enthusiasm for experiencing reality and attention to detail.'

'What above all is needed in order to educate these children? Not leaden gravity, but humour, real humour. Life-inspired humour.'

Therapeutic education goes hand in hand with therapeutic eurythmy, and comes under the Medical Section. Thirty-seven years later Professor Jacob Lutz of the University of

Cresset House near Johannesberg (South Africa)

Zürich in his text book *Child Psychiatry* (1961) had this to say about anthroposophical therapeutic education:

'For many years past I have been able to see for myself the work done in the treatment of severely mentally retarded children and children with brain damage in those homes where the methods are based on the anthroposophy of Rudolf Steiner. The help that the sick children receive there is so great, and the results of the treatment given are so significant, that they can no longer be ignored...

'I am indebted to my study of Rudolf Steiner's anthropology, pedagogy, and therapeutic education for some crucial thinking about the problems of the children to be described in this book.'

Karl König MD, who died in 1966, established the Camphill Movement for therapeutic education in Scotland, England, and South Africa. It now has village communities in many countries in which the children can grow up and spend a lifetime of activity.

AGRICULTURE

The thing that most surprised those who had followed Rudolf Steiner's career from a distance was the fact that in June 1924, immediately before the course for educational therapists, he had conducted a course of lectures for agriculturists. A spiritual scientist and initiate talking to farmers and landowners about agriculture, cattle-rearing, manuring and rotation of crops, forestry, and husbandry was really a novelty for which it would be difficult to find a parallel. In this as in all other fields, Steiner did not speak as a theorist. Those who attended the course witnessed a 'spiritual researcher' who frequently knew more about the 'things of the soil' than did they themselves, who had spent their lives coping with fields and cattle.

One can trace the origins of the peasant in Rudolf Steiner back to his childhood, when he had always to help his parents run their small garden. His characteristic reply to an over-enthusiastic admirer who after a lecture gushingly said: 'Of course, it is your profound study of philosophy that enables you to make these momentous revelations' was: 'I believe rather that what I have been able to achieve is due to the fact that as a child I learned to clean my shoes myself.'

This 'peasant' Steiner won the confidence of the farmers who came to him for advice. They formed an 'experimental circle' with the aim of putting into effect the suggestions made to them. Much was achieved in the early years. But the National Socialist period and the Second World War and its aftermath gave these efforts a temporary setback, particularly in Germany. Many estates and farms in eastern Germany which had already gone over to the new methods reverted.

This agricultural movement is today known as the *bio-dynamic method*, and its products are on sale under the Demeter trade mark, and others. This movement should not be equated with various reform movements with one restricted aim, for instance, opposition to artificial fertilizers. There is nothing negative about the recommendations made by Steiner. Their aim is to restore to a healthy condition the ravaged and poisoned earth, and its produce. In this system of agriculture, understanding of nature's economy and of the relation between earth and the cosmos is made use of to bring healing to the soil and to plant and animal life—and this includes human beings. Steiner gave the gardeners and farmers who trusted in him practical tips of which they have since made energetic use.

THE FOUNDING OF THE CHRISTIAN COMMUNITY (1921–1922)

In the confused times after the First World War the German Protestant Church was in a desperate situation. A group of young theologians and theological students turned to Rudolf Steiner for counsel and help. He had always stressed that he had no wish to become a founder of religions. Anthroposophy, as a spiritual science, is primarily concerned with the quest for knowledge and the discovery of truth, so that anyone can become a member of the Anthroposophical Society, whatever his religion. Defining the relation of his doctrine to the different faiths at Basle in 1917, Steiner stated that:

> There is no clash between anthroposophy and any one's religious faith.
>
> It is impossible to convert anthroposophy directly into religion. But anthroposophy, genuinely understood, will create a genuine, true, unfeigned religious need. For the human soul needs various paths to direct it on the way upwards to its goal. The human soul needs not only the power conferred by knowledge, it must be penetrated by that warmth that comes from the kind of contemplation of the spiritual world that is peculiar to religious faith, to true religious feeling.

In that same year of 1917 Steiner spoke on the same subject in Berlin:

> We should never behave as if the quest for spiritual knowledge were a substitute for the practice of religion and the religious life. Spiritual knowledge can greatly sustain religious life and the practice of religion, particularly in regard to the mystery of

Christ; but we should be perfectly clear that religious life and
the practice of religion within the human community kindles
the spiritual consciousness of the soul. If this spiritual consciousness is to come alive in human beings, they cannot
remain content with abstract representations of God or Christ
but will have to involve themselves again and again in the
practice of religion, in religious activity, which for every
individual can take on a different form...

The audience that listened to these words included the
most eminent preacher of the Protestant Church in Berlin:
Dr Friedrich Rittelmeyer, a deeply religious man and at the
same time a pastor of souls. In 1916 he had received a call to
the 'New Church' on the Gendarmenmarkt in Berlin from
Nuremberg, where with his friend Dr Christian Geyer he had
done great work in proclaiming the message of Jesus Christ
within the Protestant Lutheran Church. Both in Nuremberg
and in Berlin the churches in which Rittelmeyer preached
were always full to overflowing. The bound volumes of the
sermons of Geyer and Rittelmeyer, 'God and the Soul' and
'Life from God', were widely read, and copies were to be
found in many protestant homes.

In Berlin, Rittelmeyer had become a member of the
Anthroposophical Society. In 1921 he learned of the aspirations of those young theologians who had turned to Rudolf
Steiner for counsel and help in the renewal of the religious
life of the Christian church. Steiner acceded to their request
and invited the theologians to attend two courses; one at
Stuttgart at Whitsun and one at Dornach in the autumn.

These courses made a profound impression on all who
attended them. To many people's surprise, Steiner showed
himself to be a highly adept and deeply devout theologian,
who was not only aware of the ecclesiastical and ritual
problems but was also able to advise on them. Thirty years
later the Protestant theologian Paul Tillich put into these

words what Steiner had expressed: 'If the sacraments were done away with altogether, religious observance would die and the visible church would cease to exist.' But whereas Tillich looked sorrowfully on the 'death of the sacraments' and observed with resignation: 'There are no counter-forces in sight, certainly not in theology,' Steiner gave his assembled theologians detailed arguments in favour of a future sacramentalism, without which it would be impossible to build a Christian community. In a mood of deepest earnestness he reminded his hearers of the conditions necessary for such a renewal of the Christian religion, namely that the bearers and proclaimers of the message should themselves be god-inspired and should strive with every fibre of their being to lead 'a life from God'. Some of the theologians who had gathered round Rudolf Steiner accepted the admonition and the challenge. They gave up their positions and callings and placed themselves at the service of this 'movement for the renewal of religious life'. At Berlin, Marburg, and Tübingen small groups, mainly composed of students, were soon formed, and dedicated themselves enthusiastically to preparation for the life work that they were to undertake.

One year later, in September 1922, the first congregation of the Christian Community was founded at Dornach, once again with the all-important, unstinting help of Rudolf Steiner. Friedrich Rittelmeyer became its leader, with an entourage of active collaborators, mainly from the younger generation. But a few older members played a part—for instance, Prof. Hermann Beckh, an indologist from the University of Berlin, renowned for his work on Buddhism, the reverend August Pauli, one-time collaborator of Johannes Müller, and Friedrich Rittelmeyer's brother Heinrich Rittelmeyer, principal of the teachers' training college at Herford. The theologians were joined by artists, teachers, and leaders of the youth movement. All had heard

Dr Friedrich Rittelmeyer (1872–1938). Co-founder and first leader of the Christian Community

the call of the discipleship of Christ and had severed their links with their previous occupations. As though inspired by the spirit of the first Pentecost, these founders of the priesthood of the Christian Community believed that their mission was to all nations and all mankind.

The new priesthood of the Christian Community administers the Seven Sacraments in obedience to the 'Johannine Church', in the sense given to this term by Schelling and Novalis—there being no Petrine succession—rejecting all dogma and leaving the pastors free to teach and the members of the Community free to believe according to their consciences. For the first time in the history of the Christian church, in the Christian Community women as well as men serve at the altar.

The fact that the Christian Community was founded with the help of Rudolf Steiner has been a frequent cause of misunderstanding. It was never the intention to add a 'religious wing' to anthroposophy and the Anthroposophical Society. To believe this is to misunderstand both anthroposophy and the Christian Community. According to its premisses, anthroposophy is intended to be concerned with the perception of spiritual knowledge, and, if it is to be, and to remain, in the fullest sense human, the religious element must be immanent in it. The Christian Community thinks of itself as a member of the invisible Church of Christ which from its beginnings in Jerusalem and beside the Sea of Galilee has made its way in visible form for almost two thousand years via Byzantium, Rome, Geneva, Zürich, and Wittenberg, traversing the world. Though to outward appearances firmly established, this church, after passing through many transformations and reappearing in many different forms became secularized in the nineteenth century by enlightenment and liberalism. This led to the debasement

Church of the Christian Community in Berlin

of the primeval Christian impulses. Dogmatism and ortho-
doxy played their part in bringing about this decline.

But whereas all the other Christian churches and communities in their internal crises have up to the present been
conscious of Rudolf Steiner's life work as at the most a disturbing element breaking in upon their own ordered way of
life, to the founders of the Christian Community Steiner's
insight is precisely the spiritual help needed in the age of
natural science if the Church of Christ is to survive beyond
the modern world.

The Christian Community chose Stuttgart as its adminis-
trative centre. Within a few years this 'movement for the
renewal of religious life' had spread mainly to the larger
German cities. But thereafter communities were founded in
Switzerland, the Netherlands, England, Austria, Norway,
Sweden, and Czechoslovakia. Large communities such as
those at Prague, Königsberg, Danzig, Breslau, and Stettin
were destroyed in consequence of the Second World War. In
1941 the National Socialists banned the Christian Community in 'Greater Germany', the communities were dissolved,
their assets were liquidated by the Gestapo, and many of the
pastors were imprisoned.

After the war the Christian Community began to grow
unobtrusively. In Germany, first rooms were adapted as
churches, and later came church buildings. In Berlin at
Whitsun 1962 a 'new church' of the Christian Community at
Berlin-Wilmersdorf was consecrated. It was intended to
replace Rittelmeyer's 'new church', which had been
destroyed. New communities with their own pastors have
since come into being in many parts of the world.

THE FINAL YEARS

1922

The intensity of Rudolf Steiner's labours in the seven years
after the First World War that were left to him was, by
normal standards, phenomenal. As if the study and propagation of anthroposophy had not been enough to fill a lifetime, its establishment in the fields of sociology, pedagogy,
medicine and so on demanded the last ounce from him. Then
there was his involvement with the affairs of the Anthroposophical Society, whose membership had increased considerably in the short period following the war. Then, human
problems arose repeatedly, and again and again it devolved
upon Steiner to solve them. A number of student groups had
been formed at the universities and were actively advocating
the cause of anthroposophy. There was no lack of opposition
and the pros and cons were made the subject of disputes
which could not but be unwelcome to Steiner. Within the
Society, members of the German Youth Movement confronted the older members, some of whom found it hard to
leave behind them the allure of the 'theosophical' period,
with demands and revolutionary sentiments. The mood was:
'The old hands know a lot—and do little.' The young ones
'know little, but want to do a lot'. These conflicting views had
a disruptive effect within the Society. Whereas before the
war the Theosophical, later Anthroposophical, Society had
laid the main emphasis on esoteric self-contemplation,
undisturbed by the world around, it now found itself under
the necessity of facing the world, and it was mainly as a
consequence of the foundation of new establishments that
this situation came about. And there were many members

who could not cope with this. But there were also disturbing signs of a certain alienation of anthroposophical activity. Among the new members were scientists who had not sufficiently absorbed what was essentially new in anthroposophy. They brought to the work of the Society the unrefined habits of thought which belonged to the external world. Steiner was grieved that through this influence the very nature of anthroposophy began to be insidiously contaminated. Nor could narrow sectarianism and hazy mysticism be entirely rooted out.

These internal problems were matched by equally grave external ones. Owing to inflation the business enterprises of the Anthroposophical Society, which had banded together, in Switzerland under the name: 'Futurum AG' and in Germany under that of 'Der kommende Tag AG' had got into financial difficulties and had had in part to be liquidated.

Rudolf Steiner was violently assailed, above all by nationalist and orthodox religious opponents. In Munich in May 1922, on the occasion of a lecture on 'Anthroposophy and Spiritual Knowledge' at the hotel 'Vier Jahreszeiten', he was actually physically attacked by nationalist hooligans. Thanks to the courageous intervention of friends (Dr Noll, Dr Büchenbacher) he was rescued from manhandling and was able to escape through a rear door of the hotel. Unconcerned and undisturbed he went on to complete his lecture tour, which had been arranged by the Wolff and Sachs agency, in eight major German cities. But this was the portent of a further, much more severe blow.

As so often happened in Rudolf Steiner's life, the Christmas season of 1922 to 1923 was exceptionally active and busy. In a series of lectures inspired by the great medieval thinker Cardinal Nicholas of Cusa he took as his subject: 'The Historical Origins and Development of Science.' He also in the Christmas period gave four festival lectures on the 'Spiritual

Communion of Mankind', these being an elaboration of a disquisition at the end of November on the 'Relation of the Celestial Sphere to Man and of Man to the Celestial Sphere.'

On New Year's Eve 1922:

> What at any other time would be abstract knowledge becomes a relation of the feelings and the will with the world. The world becomes the House of God. The man of perception ... becomes the sacrificer...
>
> This is today's great task; to note around us the mood of the dying year, how all passes away and perishes, and yet how in those in whose hearts resides the consciousness of true humanity, god-like humanity, the spirit of the New Year must be alive, the spirit of a new era and of rebirth.

The last words of the new year address had died away. The audience had all left. An eye witness has described what followed: 'Shortly afterwards the caretaker saw smoke and operated the alarm to summon the Goetheanum fire brigade, who arrived promptly. Smoke in the 'white room', was the report. All the rooms in the south wing were opened up and searched. No fire was detected in any of them. Smoke was penetrating from the western outer wall of the south wing. A breach was immediately made in this wall, and the structure within it was found to be in flames. When the alarm reached the ... neighbouring houses, we raced up the hill. In a matter of minutes many water hoses had been laid, the flat roof climbed, and the heart of the fire deluged with water. We still believed that it would be possible to hem the fire in and extinguish it, the fire brigade, with hundreds of helpers, fearlessly risked their lives. But the ominous smoke welled thicker and thicker from the south wing. We burst in ... In the hall under the big dome we were met by the roar of the flames which were consuming everything in the space between the walls. Anything that could be carried away was

The ruins of the first Goetheanum, 1923

rescued. But soon the smoke became so dense that it was
impossible to breathe. A voice passed on to us Rudolf
Steiner's order to leave the building. The fire had triumphed
over human wills ... Around midnight the domes collapsed,
and at 7 in the morning the mighty pillars were still burning.
That night, Rudolf Steiner walked round and round the
building in silence. Once only he was heard to say: "Much
work and many years." Until morning he stood before the
ruined building in silence, his only concern lest the life of
anyone should be endangered. His greatness, dignity, and
goodness gave us the strength that night to bear it all. When
New Year's morning dawned he said: "We will continue to
do our self-imposed duty in the premises that are still left to
us".'

The fruits of ten years' mental and physical labour had
fallen victim to an arsonist. The conference was continued on
the following day without interruption and without omis-
sions, in the neighbouring joinery shop, where all the
woodwork for the Goetheanum had been put together.

At the appointed time Steiner appeared on a hurriedly erected rostrum and announced: 'We will continue with the lectures as planned.' Even a twelfth-night play that had been planned was performed

1923

Rudolf Steiner was deeply grieved at the destruction of the first Goetheanum. The loss was in the literal sense of the word irreplaceable for both him and anthroposophy. It was impossible to restore the entire structure, with its interior built from a variety of woods and its domes with their painted ceilings. As a unique expression of the artistic impulse that inspired Rudolf Steiner, they were no more.

There were those among the members in whom stirred the wish to rebuild. But at the same time it was clear that the good intentions were surrounded by a good deal of self-deception. Steiner had been greatly troubled by things that had happened in the most recent phase of the Society's development. The ruins of the Goetheanum that he contemplated every day were something more than a sign to him that there were those in the world who were opposed to anthroposophy and who would not stop short at arson. He also sensed in the pile of ruins a warning that the Society of recent years 'had lost its inner cohesion and that there was something ruinous about it'. For this reason there could be for him no rebuilding unless it was linked with the renewal of the Anthroposophical Society from within. 'There is no sense in rebuilding unless the Anthroposophical Society which stands behind the project is sure of itself, attentive to its duty, and strong.'

In 1923 he was concerned first and foremost with this reform and with the advancement of the Waldorf School in Stuttgart. He attempted to prevail on the German anthro-

Rudolf Steiner, 1923

posophists, in the first instance, to pause for reflection and look back on the numerous errors that had been committed in recent years. He made no less than 18 visits to Stuttgart, now without question the centre of anthroposophy in Germany.

He sometimes had some hard things to say—as he himself admits. But he also made journeys to Prague, Oslo, England, and the Netherlands with the same object principally in mind. On the occasion of the general meeting of the Anthroposophical Society in Switzerland he gave a series of eight lectures the subject of which was: 'The History and Circumstances of the Anthroposophical Movement in Relation to the Anthroposophical Society' in which he told the members of all the things that he expected of them if the Society was to be restored to a sound condition. His demands included an end to all sectarianism, a matter-of-fact attitude to life in all its aspects, and the courage to resist any debasement of anthroposophy. There must be truly serious concern for the spiritual, which to the anthroposophist is not a theoretical construct but an invisible, living essence. 'Then, possibly, there will be less said about brotherhood, about love of humanity in general, but there will be all the more love in our hearts, and from the very tone of voice in which people say what it is that holds them to anthroposophy' it will be seen in what manner they serve the invisible essence, Anthroposophy.

The restoration of health at which he aims can be achieved, he says, 'if anthroposophists display so refined a sense of truth and actuality that people will observe: that is an anthroposophist; we see that he has such a refined instinct for going no further in his assertions than will square with reality.'

In the year 1923, Rudolf Steiner must have had many grave matters to ponder over. We know that he considered severing his connection with the Anthroposophical Society altogether and withdrawing with just a few of his closest followers. The decision to do the opposite and to associate himself with that society much more closely than before must have been a difficult one to make.

The Christmas Foundation Conference

At Christmas 1923 almost 800 members thronged to the hill of Dornach from every quarter. The joinery shop close to the ruins barely sufficed to hold the audiences that assembled daily. The heating arrangements were quite inadequate. But all this in no way detracted from what all those present regarded as a spiritual experience, and on which all the followers of Rudolf Steiner still look back with awe.

When the Anthroposophical Society was founded in 1913, Rudolf Steiner had not officially joined it. He was an adviser and teacher to the Society but neither a member nor a leader of it.

Now, ten years later, he himself founded the *General Anthroposophical Society*, of which the societies in the various countries were to be autonomous members. And he became its President.

In his inaugural lecture his opening question was: 'At this Christmas congress, where do we start from, and what have we learned from experience, in the ten years since the Anthroposophical Society was founded?'

The gist of his answers was:

1. It would only be possible to continue if he formally took over the leadership himself and accepted the responsibility that this entailed.

2. The General Anthroposophical Society was to be a world-wide society with its centre in the Goetheanum at Dornach.

3. The Society must open its doors to the world, so that all can be members who desire to seek and understand anthroposophy... 'The Anthroposophical Society is not a secret society, but an entirely open one. Anyone may become a member, whatever his country, social standing, religion, scientific or artistic conviction, provided that he accepts that there is some justification for the existence of an institution such as the Goetheanum at Dornach as a free school of spiritual science (§ 4 of the Statutes).

4. The statutes, which are essential for such a society, should describe only what is factual. 'These Statutes are attuned to what is purely human. Principles ... dogma play no part in them. They state ...: Here in Dornach is the Goetheanum. This Goetheanum is run in a certain way. In the Goetheanum it is sought to do such and such work...'

It might be thought that these are secondary matters. But to Steiner they were not without importance. He knew only

Rudolf Steiner, 1923

*Albert Steffen (1884–1963)
in 1927*

too well how little it costs to draw up impressive-sounding programmes, Statutes, and so on. But in relation to these matters he was all the more concerned for honesty, truth to fact, and humanity. His aim was at all costs to shun all verbiage.

5. 'The spirit of the present age demands full publicity for everything that happens. And a society which is established on firm foundations must not act contrary to the spirit of the age ... And thus today we can do no other than claim for the General Anthroposophical Society, which it is our intention to found, a full measure of publicity.'

Up to this time the printed texts of many of Rudolf Steiner's lectures had been accessible only to members. Since the Christmas Conference, everybody has been able to obtain them from the book trade.

6. Man of today has no use for dogma, he rejects sectarianism. His instinct is right. But there is no denying 'that

within the Anthroposophical Society it is difficult to shake off this sectarianism. But shaken off it must be. There must be no shred of it in the new Anthroposophical Society of the future. It must be in truth a world society.'

7. Promoting anthroposophy by stealth is bad and will do harm. Whatever is new and unusual about anthroposophy in all fields, such as eurythmy, speech-training, and medicine should be defended with courage.

These were all points made by Steiner in his inaugural speech on 24 December. There followed eight days during which the 'foundation stone' of the General Anthroposophical Society was laid, whereby the life of the Anthroposophical Society was enriched by an entirely new element.

At the same time that the Society was being restructured from without and from within, the School of Spiritual Science was founded. 'The establishment of the School of Spiritual Science is first and foremost the responsibility of Rudolf Steiner, who is to appoint his collaborators and his successor.' (§ 7 of the Statutes).

It is here stated in unmistakeable terms that he is prepared to occupy personally this position which is central to all the anthroposophical work. A further Statute (§ 9) lays down the linking together of the Society and the School:

'The purpose of the Anthroposophical Society is to promote spiritual research. The purpose of the School of Spiritual Science is to conduct that research. The Anthroposophical Society shall reject dogmatism in any field whatsoever.'

A committee under the chairmanship of Rudolf Steiner was formed to conduct the affairs of the General Anthroposophical Society. Its members, working together were responsible for the running of the various Sections of the School as follows:

The Swiss poet Albert Steffen became deputy Chairman and Leader of the Section for Literature. 'If we are to have a Swiss as committee member and Deputy Chairman of the Anthroposophical Society, one could not have a better one than this.'

Frau Marie Steiner, who was jointly responsible for the first founding of the Anthroposophical Society in 1913, headed the Section for the Spoken Arts and Music.

Ita Wegman MD, a Dutch physician, conducted the Medical Section, in which the Arlesheim Clinic was incorporated.

Dr Elisabeth Vreede, who was also Dutch, headed the Section for Mathematics and Astronomy.

Dr Guenther Wachsmuth, the secretary and treasurer of the Society, headed the Science Section.

This re-founding of the Society and the School was linked to Rudolf Steiner's purpose of establishing in the West for the first time, in the full blaze of publicity, a modern Christian 'abode of the mysteries' from whence should issue forces for the stimulation and healing, of art, science, and religion, to the benefit of the life of Man. Empty phrases, habit, sham pathos, enthusiastic gushing, and mysticism were rigorously excised. From now on, the activities of the Society were to be permeated by the truly 'esoteric', which always is identical with the truly 'human'. Rudolf Steiner sought to achieve this lofty aim less with words than by action through personal involvement in the setting up of the new establishments. The conference had been planned in association with the Christmas festival. A constant feature of it was the following mantra, which Rudolf Steiner recited daily:

> Light,
> Warming the hearts
> Of the poor shepherds;

Light,
Enlightening
The wise heads of kings.

Divine light,
Sun of Christ
Warm our hearts;
Enlighten
Our heads;
Prosper
That which we
From our hearts
And with our minds
Of set purpose
Seek to achieve.

1924/1925

On 1 January 1924, exactly one year after the fire, the Christmas Foundation Conference drew to its close. Only nine months were left to Rudolf Steiner to complete what had been begun. An ailment that first manifested itself on the evening of this first day of January, and that until the autumn he again and again mastered, compelled him in the last days of September to take to his sickbed, from which he was never to rise again. But these nine months saw a further intensification of his activity. In stating that in the short time left to him he gave 338 lectures and 68 addresses, discussions, and meetings at which he answered questions—all this in the space of 272 days—we are talking of the external circumstances. But behind these external circumstances there is a spiritual reality that is a matter for amazement. Every word of these lectures was taken down in shorthand, and nearly all of this is available in book form today, so that anyone who is

interested can follow a daily record of how abundantly
Rudolf Steiner laboured at that time. Was it, as he himself
suggested, a recompense made by the spiritual world for the
loss caused to anthroposophy by the burning down of the
Goetheanum? Was it the imminence of death that gave him
this abundance of spiritual potentialities?

Immediately after the Christmas Conference Steiner held
a course for 'young medical men', which the doctors and
medical students who attended it found particularly inspiring.
He not only imparted knowledge about spiritual science to
them, but tried to develop in full measure that in the personality of those who practise the art of healing which one
may call the moral and esoteric mentality of the doctor.

For years Steiner had at regular intervals given lectures to
the workers engaged in the construction of the Goetheanum
on practical and intellectual problems. These were very
popular with the workers. He could speak the kind of language that simple people understand. Even in 1924 physical
weakness and excess of other work did not prevent his doing
this work, which he saw and loved as a social obligation.
These lectures are now available in book form, so that anyone who wishes to do so can form his own impressions about
them.

It was at this time that he made the model for the second
Goetheanum. This building was not dedicated until three
years after his death. Although in a quite different way, its
style differs considerably from the present tradition. Allow-
ing for the difference in the building materials used—the
first building was made of wood and the second one of concrete—a structure arose which, despite its austere forms,
merges well with the Dornach landscape, in the foothills of
the Swiss Jura.

Like a living intelligent being the Goetheanum stands,
facing west into the setting sun. Inexorably and sternly it

appears to be asking: Can the West, to whose lot it fell through technology to spread death to culture over the earth, find the strength to turn this decline into a reawakening?

In these days Rudolf Steiner exerted his powers to the absolute limit. Those around him wondered when he found time to sleep. After everyone had gone to rest, the light still burned in his room, they knew that he was at work—and in the morning he was always the first to arrive.

And so in these months the educational therapy and agricultural movements were started, teachers, exponents of eurythmy, and medical men received their final, all-important stimulus, the Christian Community was given vital aid. He made journeys to Prague, Paris, the Netherlands, and England and took there with him the impact of the Christmas Conference.

It seemed as though Rudolf Steiner had ventured on to a new plane of spiritual existence and was now able to give expression to that which, while it had long been stored up within him, was only now ripe for utterance. The lecture series during the Christmas Conference, *World History in the Light of Anthroposophy*, was the introduction to the 'karma lectures' which were continued right through these months up to the last day.

The belief that an individual must undergo incarnation at intervals of time in order to make compensation for the past in a new life on earth and to mature by encountering new experience, is as old as time. For millennia it has dominated the spiritual life of the Orient—may it not have been the first belief ever formulated? These doctrines have always limited themselves to general terms. To our knowledge, Rudolf Steiner was the first who was so bold as actually to trace, through his spiritual research, the currents of world history and the lives of individuals through long periods of time, and to present the results of this research to a large audience.

None of those who heard him was in a position to check in every detail the truth of what he related. But all of us to whom Steiner communicated the results of his spiritual research formed the impression that in prospecting this new field of research he proceeded with the same diligence, accuracy, and reliability, as we are accustomed to, and ought to demand of, the best researchers of our time in, say, physics or astronomy.

Between 20 January and 10 August, eighteen *Letters to Members* from Rudolf Steiner appeared in the periodical published by the Anthroposophical Society. In these he tried

Draft of page 1 of Mein Lebensgang, *Rudolf Steiner's auto-biography, 1923*

to convey to the members what the Christmas Conference was all about, spiritually speaking:

> Anthroposophy can only thrive if it really lives. For the central feature of anthroposophy is life. It is life emanating from the spirit...
>
> The original form in which it can come among human beings is the idea; and the first entrance through which it approaches them is reason. If this were not so, it would have no content. It would be mere gushing sentiment. But true spirit does not enthuse, it speaks a language that is clear and meaningful.

These letters to the members led up to the 'Leading Thoughts' which were later published with the title *The Michael Mystery*. Steiner wrote the greater part of these leading thoughts on his sickbed, and they appeared in weekly instalments until the last week of March 1925. In them he described for the last time, and from a new vantage point, the essential nature of anthroposophy and its mission.

On his return from England at the beginning of September, more than a thousand people were waiting for him at Dornach, among them being doctors, actors, and theologians for whom he had promised to give special courses. Although his sickness was already heavy upon him he kept all his promises and spoke without a break for three weeks to audiences of actors, elocutionists, teachers, and so on on 'speech formation and dramatic art,' to the theologians of the Christian Community about the Apocalypse of John, and to doctors and priests about pastoral medicine. The usual lectures for the workers at the Goetheanum, for all the members, and for the pupils of the School of Spiritual Science were continued without interruption until the 28 of September. Overwork—it has been reckoned that in the final three weeks he received almost 400 private visitors who had come to him for advice—had put too great a strain upon his powers. Immediately after delivering his last address on St. Michael's Eve, he was compelled to take to his bed. Under the care of his medical friends, Dr Ita Wegmann and Dr Ludwig Noll, even from his sickbed he continued to be intensely active, mainly through the medium of the written word. His bed was in his studio, at the foot of the uncompleted statue of Christ. The studio was annexed to the joiner's shop and had thus escaped the flames.

Many people had urged Rudolf Steiner to write his auto-biography, and in December 1923 he began to set down, in instalments which appeared weekly, what was later to be published under the title *Mein Lebensgang* and is now known in English as *Autobiography. Chapters in the Course of my Life.* Even during his illness this work went on without interruption. To every instalment the words 'To be con-tinued' in his own hand-writing are added, but the final manuscript, which he sent to the printer's in the last week of March 1925, does not have these words added.

The new Goetheanum (completed 1928–29)

And so he lay there in his studio, bound by sickness but with his mind indefatigably at work. 'He liked to hear the bustling noise of the hammering and fitting out that penetrated the stillness of his sickroom from the site where the Goetheanum was being built and that told its own story of the structure that was being raised.' To the last, every fibre of his being drew him to the new Centre for Anthroposophy now being erected, and to its human upholders: the Society and its members. And so came the 30 of March. Guenther Wachsmuth, who was present, writes:

'Rudolf Steiner's last moments on earth were free of all physical struggle, free of all the uncertainty that attends the death of so many men, his face bespoke peace, grace, inner certainty, spiritual vision. He folded his hands across his breast, his eyes were bright and his gaze was directed towards spheres with which in vision he saw himself united. As he drew his last breath, he closed his eyes himself. The impression that this made in the room was, not that this was the end but that it was action on a high spiritual plane. His features, his hands in an attitude expressive of the power of prayer, revealed exalted, radiant awareness. Just as the great artists contrive to create the impression that the knights lying in repose on the sarcophagi from the Middle Ages can still see through their closed eyelids, that their reposing figures can still stride onwards, so here the figure lying at rest expressed supernatural awareness, a journeying in the realms of the spirit.'

POSTSCRIPT

A dense cloud hangs over European civilization, and truly it is only in a way surprising how little people in general are willing to allow themselves ... to feel and to be aware of this dense cloud.

Rudolf Steiner, 1924

When Rudolf Steiner died, little more than the foundations of the second Goetheanum existed. What the master had devised and planned, his apprentices and journeymen had to execute without his aid.

At the moment when all had been set on track once again but nothing had been brought to a conclusion, the Society and the School of Spiritual Science had lost their leader. It was often more than the 'pupils' could cope with; the work that the 'teacher' had planned, and that was to span the world, was too vast in scale.

It is the nature of the person studying anthroposophy and seeking to live by it, his personality, that gives it individuality and determines the face that it presents to the world. Working to a set pattern negates the aims of anthroposophy. No wonder that shortly after the death of Rudolf Steiner the Anthroposophical Society passed through a series of crises. To make matters worse, for ten years under Hitler it was banned in Germany, the land of its birth. But in all these trials it has proved itself extremely viable and has to a great extent overcome its initial difficulties. After the death of Rudolf Steiner, Albert Steffen became president of the Society. The original executive members have since died: Ita Wegman and Elisabeth Vreede in 1943, Marie Steiner in 1948, Guenther Wachsmuth and Albert Steffen in 1963.

Every year, thousands of members, and others who are interested, visit the Goetheanum, the main object being to see the performances of the four Mystery Plays, the plays of Albert Steffen, and the production of Goethe's *Faust*. (The Goetheanum is today the only place on earth where one can see both parts of *Faust* presented unabridged.) The annual reports of the Goetheanum contain references to an abundance of lectures, seminars, and artistic events. The clinic at Arlesheim with the Institute for Cancer Research and the factories of Weleda AG have been extended. Every year the number of schools and of establishments for therapeutic education increases throughout the world. A staff is engaged in studying the literary remains, with the principal object of publishing the complete works of Rudolf Steiner.

Looking at the life and work of Rudolf Steiner, one is tempted to ask the present generation, which knows that it is on the edge of an abyss: Who and what do you seek? Do you wish to conquer materialism? To solve the social question? Do you aim at the rebirth of science, art, and religion? Rudolf Steiner has given his answers to all these questions. Events have not turned out as expected. Is this sufficient reason for rejecting his answers? Because the language he uses is so unusual? Because many of his followers fail to carry conviction? In the old days, did the great prophets and leaders of humanity fare any differently? Has our generation taken the trouble to give him and his work a fair test? Has it given a fair hearing to what he had to say, or taken up and tested his many suggestions? A monograph on Rudolf Steiner, written in the second half of the twentieth century, cannot but end by asking some severely searching questions.

CHRONOLOGY

The figures in square brackets show the approximate number of anthroposophical lectures given in the year, followed in round brackets by the approximate number of talks, addresses, funeral orations, question & answer sessions, discussions with teachers and other groups, introductions to eurythmy performances etc.

EARLY LIFE: 1861–1879

Childhood and Youth

1861   Born 27 February 1861 at Kraljevec, then in Hungary, now in Croatia. Father Johann Steiner (1829–1910) was an official of the Austrian Südbahn (Southern Railway). Both parents came from the 'Forest District' of Lower Austria.

1862   Father transferred briefly to Mödling near Vienna.

From 1863   Childhood at Pottschach, a station on the Semmering Railway (Styria).

From 1868   Youth at Neudörfl on the Leitha (Burgenland).

1872   Attended the modern school at Wiener-Neustadt.

1879   Passed school-leaving examination with distinction.

SECOND PERIOD: AUTUMN 1879–1890

Student Years in Vienna

1879   Father transferred to Inzersdorf near Vienna. Student at the Technical University. Principal subjects: mathematics, biology, physics, chemistry. Teachers in the humanities: Karl Julius Schröer (German literature), Robert Zimmermann and Franz Brentano (philosophy), Otto Karl Lorenz (history). Fundamental study of Goethe.

1882   Aged 21, commissioned to edit Goethe's scientific writings for Kürschner's *National-Litteratur*.

1886   Book on Goethe's world view.
1888   Editorship of the *Deutsche Wochenschrift*. Lecture on
          Goethe to the Vienna Goethe Society.
1889   First visits to Weimar, Eisenach and Berlin. Contract
          with Suphan.

THIRD PERIOD: 1890–1896

Weimar Years

1890   Move to Weimar in the autumn. Regular collaborator
          at the Goethe and Schiller Archives. Edited the
          Sophia Edition of Goethe's scientific writings.
          Acquaintance with Herman Grimm, von Loeper,
          Erich Schmidt, Heinrich von Treitschke, Hermann
          Helmholtz, Ernst Haeckel. Friendship with Ludwig
          Laistner and Gabriele Reuter. First acquaintance with
          Otto Erich Hartleben.
1891   Doctor of Philosophy degree at Rostock University
          under Professor Heinrich von Stein.
1894   Wrote *Die Philosophie der Freiheit* (*The Philosophy of
          Freedom*). Visit to the ailing Friedrich Nietzsche at
          Naumburg. Meeting with Fritz Koegel and Elisabeth
          Förster-Nietzsche.
1895   Book on Nietzsche.
1897   Book on Goethe's world view.

FOURTH PERIOD: 1897–1901

Berlin, Early Years

1897   Move to Berlin.
1897–1900 Joint editor with Otto Erich Hartleben of *Magazin für
          Litteratur* and its supplement *Dramaturgische Blätter*.
          Active in the Independent Literary Society and the
          Independent Dramatic Society, in the circle of 'Die
          Kommenden' ('The Coming Generation'), at the
          Independent Academy and in the Giordano Bruno
          Federation. Friendship with John Henry Mackay and

Ludwig Jacobowski; contacts with Bruno Wille and Wilhelm Bölsche.

1899　On 31 October, marriage to Anna, formerly Eunike, née Schultz (b. Beelitz, 8 May 1853).

1899–1904　Teacher at the Workers' Educational Institute: lectures, courses, elocution training.

1900　Book on Haeckel. Lectures and participation in a commemoration of Nietzsche at the Association for the Promotion of Art. Lecture to the Association for Academic Teaching. Other Nietzsche commemoration events. On the occasion of the Gutenberg Quincentenary, address to 7000 typesetters and printers in a Berlin circus (17 June). Early lectures at the Theosophical Library in the house of Count and Countess Brockdorff.

1901　Further lectures at the Theosophical Library. Address at the commemoration of the foundation of the Association for Women and Girls of the Working Class (9 March). Funeral oration for Ludwig Jacobowski (9 May). Lectures to 'The Coming Generation'. Lecture on Hegel to students of the Technical University (22 November).

FIFTH PERIOD: 1902–1923

The Development of Anthroposophy

First phase in the development of anthroposophy: 1902–1909

1902　Wrote *Das Christentum als mystische Tatsache* (*Christianity as Mystical Fact*). Joined the Theosophical Society. Continuation of work at the Workers' Educational Institute, at the Theosophical Library, in the circle of 'The Coming Generation' and in the Giordano Bruno Federation. Together with Marie von Sivers, attended the 13th annual convention of the European Section of the Theosophical Society in London (July). Founding of the German section of the Theosophical Society (October) with Rudolf Steiner as General Secretary. Lectures to the Independent Academy. A 'Ferdinand Freiligrath Evening' at the Schiller Theatre. Editor of journal *Lucifer*, subsequently *Lucifer-Gnosis*.

1903   Activities in Berlin continue as hitherto until 1914. Commencement of public work in support of theosophy in Weimar, Cologne and Hamburg. Tegel (Berlin): Address beside the Humboldt graves at a celebration of the Giordano Bruno Federation. Visit to London.

1904   Wrote *Theosophie* (*Theosophy*) and *Wie erlangt man Erkenntnisse der höheren Welten?* (*How to Know the Higher Worlds*). As well as continuing to lecture at the Berlin Workers' Educational Institute, lectured in several other German towns and at the Theosophical Congress in Amsterdam. [215 (74 mainly talks at the Workers' Educational Institute)]

1905   His address on the occasion of the twelfth anniversary of the founding of the Workers' Educational Institute (22 January) marked the end of Rudolf Steiner's work there. Expansion of activities of the Theosophical Society in Berlin, lecturing there and in the principal cities of Germany, and also in London and Switzerland. [228 (9)]

1906   The first important lecture series outside Berlin: in Paris. First meeting with Edouard Schuré. Founding of branches of the Theosophical Society in Frankfurt am Main and Bremen, also elsewhere. Lectures in other German cities and in Switzerland. [244 (6)]

1907   Lectures in many German cities, especially Munich. Also in Switzerland, Vienna, Prague and Budapest. [198 (6)]

1908   Two lecture tours in Scandinavia in addition to many lectures in German cities, Holland, Switzerland, Vienna and Prague. [239 (8)]

1909   First meeting with Christian Morgenstern in Berlin. First reference to the second coming of Christ. Lecture series in many German cities as well as Strasbourg, Oslo, Budapest, Vienna and several Swiss towns. [224 (9)]

Second phase in the development of anthroposophy: 1910-1916

1910   Wrote *Die Geheimwissenschaft im Umriss* (*An Outline of Esoteric Science*). Lectured in many German cities as well as in Stockholm, Strasbourg, Vienna, Rome, Copenhagen, Oslo, and Switzerland. Munich: performance of the first mystery drama. [207 (7)]

1911   19 March: death of Anna Steiner. Lectures in many German cities, as well as in Prague, Copenhagen, Sweden, Oslo, Switzerland and Italy (International Congress of Philosophers at Bologna). Munich: performance of the second mystery drama. [165 (7)]

1912   September saw the beginnings of eurythmy and preparations for the founding of the Anthroposophical Society. Lectures in many German cities as well as Vienna, Helsinki, Stockholm, Prague, Copenhagen, Oslo, Switzerland and Italy. Munich: performance of the third mystery drama. [157 (8)]

1913   2–3 February: institution of the Anthroposophical Society. Lectures in Germany, Switzerland, Austria, Holland, Paris, Helsinki and Oslo. 20 September: Laying of the foundation stone of the first Goetheanum at Dornach. Munich: performance of the fourth mystery drama. [165 (25)]

1914–1923   Resident alternately in Dornach and Berlin.

1914   31 March: death of Christian Morgenstern. 1 April: topping-out ceremony for the first Goetheanum. Lectures in Germany, Vienna, Prague, Paris (Chartres) and Sweden, from August in Dornach. July: as war broke out Steiner was attending the *Parsifal* festival at Bayreuth. 24 December: marriage to Marie von Sivers. [116 (20)]

1915–1916 Work on the Goetheanum continued.
1915   Lectures in Germany, Austria, Dornach and else-
            where in Switzerland, Prague. September: first course
            of lectures on speech eurythmy. [159 (14)]
1916   Lectures in Dornach and elsewhere in Switzerland,
            and in Germany. [145 (7)]

Third phase in the development of anthroposophy: 1917-1923
1917   Lecture series in Berlin, Dornach and elsewhere in
            Switzerland. [133 (9)]
1918   From mid-January resident in Berlin; the latter half
            of the year in Dornach. Movement for the threefold
            organization of society. Lectures in Dornach, else-
            where in Switzerland, Germany and Vienna. [152
            (14)]
1919   Lecture series at Dornach on social questions.
            Memorandum: *An das deutsche Volk und an die Kul-
            turwelt* (To the German people and the civilized
            world). Book: *Kernpunkte der sozialen Frage*
            (Towards Social Renewal) Address to the workers at
            Bosch, Delmonte and Daimler-Werke. Stuttgart:
            founding of the Waldorf School; lecture courses and
            seminars on education. Lectures in Dornach, else-
            where in Switzerland, and Germany. Performances of
            Goethe's *Faust* at the Goetheanum. [268 (80)]
1920   Lectures at Dornach. Constant contributions to the
            Waldorf School work, especially regular attendance at
            the teachers' meetings (1919–1924). First and second
            lecture series on science. Lectures on speech. Lectures
            for physicians and medical students. Lectures on
            education in Basle. [241 (155)]
1921   Lecture series in Stuttgart, and course on speech. Visit
            to Holland. Lecture series in Stuttgart. Second medi-
            cal course. Lectures on therapeutic eurythmy. First
            and second course for theologians. Academic course
            in Darmstadt. Public lectures in Oslo to the Educa-
            tional Union, the Theological Association and the

Economic Association, among others. Dornach: lectures to teachers. [302 (102)]

1922   Academic course in Berlin. Stratford on Avon: Shakespeare celebrations. Vienna: West-East Congress. Dornach: lectures on political economy. Oxford: holiday conference on spiritual values in education and social life. September: founding of the Christian Community. *Semaines Françaises*. Lectures to young people in Stuttgart. Lectures in Holland. [208 (116)]

1922/23   New Year's Eve: Destruction of the first Goetheanum by arson.

1923   Restructuring the Anthroposophical Society from within: preparations in Germany, Norway, Switzerland, Britain, Holland, Austria towards the founding of the General Anthroposophical Society. Lectures at Dornach, in Germany, Prague, Paris, Penmaenmawr, Torquay and London. [296 (171)]

1923–24   25 December–1 January: The Christmas Conference of the General Anthroposophical Society. Foundation of the School of Spiritual Science.

1923–1925   In the journal *Das Goetheanum*: weekly instalments of *Mein Lebensgang*, Rudolf Steiner's *Autobiography*. Also *Letters to Members* and *Anthroposophical Leading Thoughts*.

THE FINAL YEARS 1924–1925

1924   Lectures to young doctors and medical students at Dornach. Lectures on karma at Dornach, Prague, Berne, Breslau, Arnhem, London. Dornach: course on music eurythmy. Koberwitz (Silesia): course on agriculture. Dornach: Course on speech eurythmy. More lectures to the workers at the Goetheanum. Dornach: course on speech and dramatic art. Dornach: final course for theologians, on the Book of Revelation. 28 September: last address to members of the Anthroposophical Society. [First 9 months of the year 344 (84)]

1925   30 March: death of Rudolf Steiner.
            Publication of: *Grundlegendes für eine Erweiterung
            der Heilkunst* (*Extending Practical Medicine. Funda-
            mental Principles based on the Science of the Spirit*),
            written in collaboration with Ita Wegman.
1943   4 March: death of Ita Wegman MD.
1948   27 March: death of Marie Steiner, née von Sivers.
1963   13 July: death of Albert Steffen, Rudolf Steiner's
            successor as President of the General Anthro-
            posophical Society.

For a day by day record of Rudolf Steiner's lectures see Hans
Schmidt *Das Vortragswerk Rudolf Steiners*, Philosophisch-
Anthroposophischer Verlag, Dornach Switzerland.

SOME TRIBUTES

RUSSEL W. DAVENPORT

If man's faith could be regenerated, the palpable disintegration of western civilization could be halted. But this 'if' raises some fundamental questions. The first question is, why men have lost their faith? And, supposing this question to be answered: how could such a faith be created?

This second question gives me cause to render thanks to two masters who so closely resemble each other in their thinking that they may be considered as one. The first is Johann Wolfgang von Goethe (1749–1832) and the second his most distinguished interpreter, Rudolf Steiner (1861–1925). It may seem a matter for surprise that in making this acknowledgement of an exceptional spiritual debt I should link these two names, for Goethe is renowned above all as a poet and writer, and Steiner is regarded as a mystic whose work appears to be incomprehensible and quite out of touch with our age. But anyone who is familiar with the writings of these two men will understand why we feel ourselves to be particularly indebted to them.

One of the intellectual curiosities of the 20th century is that the academic world has seen fit to consider that Steiner's works have no foundation and are of no significance. But whoever takes it upon himself to study his voluminous works (at least a hundred publications) with an open mind will find himself in the presence of one of the greatest thinkers of all time, whose mastery of modern sciences is as wonderful as is his knowledge of the sciences of antiquity. Steiner is no more a mystic than Albert Einstein; he was first and foremost a scientist, but 'a scientist who had the daring to penetrate the mysteries of life'.

The linking of Goethe with Steiner brings us back to the question: by what means can faith be revived in the 20th century?

Rudolf Steiner's answer is: faith can only be brought back into our lives again through progress in the field of knowledge.

The Dignity of Man, 1955

A. P. SHEPHERD

The one answer that could resolve the present-day confusion of humanity would have to be a scientific exposition of the universe and of man that would do justice to the instinctive trust of man in the unquestioned value of the individual personality and would see religion as complementary to this conception, not by denying the supernatural claims of religion but by giving them their place in the scientific order of the universe. To most scientists it seemed impossible that such an answer could be found, and many religious thinkers considered the attempt presumptuous.

The fact is that such an answer has been provided by a man whose thinking is to a great extent scientifically grounded, who thought, spoke, and wrote in all respects as a scientist. This man was Rudolf Steiner.

A Scientist of the Invisible, 1954

BRUNO WALTER

In old age I have had the good fortune to be initiated into the world of anthroposophy and during the past few years to make a profound study of the teachings of Rudolf Steiner. Here we see alive and in operation that deliverance of which Hölderlin speaks; its blessing has flowed over me, and so this book is the confession of belief in anthroposophy. There is no part of my inward life that has not had new light shed upon it, or been stimulated, by the lofty teachings of Rudolf Steiner ... I am profoundly grateful for having been so boundlessly enriched ... It is glorious to become a learner again at my time of life. I have a sense of the rejuvenation of my whole being which gives strength and renewal to my musicianship, even to my music-making.

Von der Musik und vom Musizieren, 1957

CHRISTIAN MORGENSTERN

When it falls to the lot of his first biographer to recount the life of this great man, then, and only then, will the full extent of Rudolf Steiner's achievements and their, in the highest human sense, creative nature be revealed. Then people will view with profound amazement what is happening and what has happened to humanity, and what irreplaceable strength and support it has received from this man's mind while this age hurtles onwards into the terrifying wasteland of materialism.

SELMA LAGERLÖF

This man is a striking phenomenon, which we should endeavour to take seriously. He proclaims some doctrines in which I have long believed; one such doctrine is that it is not for our age to offer a religion which is full of unsubstantiated miracles: rather should religion be a science, susceptible of proof; it is no longer a question of believing, but of *knowing*. A further doctrine is that it is possible to attain to knowledge of the spiritual world by firm, conscious, systematic thought. A man should not sit like a mystic wrapt in dreams, but should exert his intellectual powers to the full in the endeavour to see the world that is hidden from us. This is true and just: and then everything about him carries conviction, and he is wise, without a hint of the charlatan. In years to come, this doctrine will be proclaimed from the pulpits.

LUDWIG BERGER

There was another name besides that of Emil Bock, an all-important name, the foremost: Rudolf Steiner. His biblical research and exegesis aroused in me a love that had all but died. It is to him that I owe it that, since those wartime nights, Nathaniel the Israelite, Nicodemus, who came by night, and Lazarus, whom the Lord loved, became real to me, and that finally I was able to understand something that gave the tales of these encounters a sense that was credible. While the bombs burst outside, within myself a hymn of reverence arose. In our youth Johann Sebastian

Bach gave us the Gospels, long before we could grasp what it was that we loved. During those nights, Rudolf Steiner opened the Bible to me once more.

Summe eines Lebens, 1953

FURTHER READING

Basic Books on Anthroposophy by Rudolf Steiner

Year written shown in square brackets.
GA = *Gesamtausgabe*, the collected works of Rudolf Steiner in the original German.

The Philosophy of Freedom. A Philosophy of Spiritual Activity (GA 4) [1894]. Rudolf Steiner Press, London 1988.
Christianity as Mystical Fact and the Mysteries of Antiquity (GA 8) [1902]. Anthroposophic Press, Hudson 1992.
Theosophy. An Introduction to the Spiritual Processes in Human Life and in the Cosmos (GA 9) [1904]. Rudolf Steiner Press, London 1994.
How to Know Higher Worlds. A Modern Path of Initiation (GA 10) [1904/05]. Anthroposophic Press, Hudson 1994.
An Outline of Esoteric Science (GA 13) [1910]. Anthroposophic Press, Hudson 1997.

Selection of Lectures and Courses by Rudolf Steiner

Venues and dates of lectures shown in square brackets.

Founding a Science of the Spirit (GA 95) [Stuttgart 1906]. Rudolf Steiner Press, London 1999.
Anthroposophy in Everyday Life [various venues, between 1909 and 1912]. Anthroposophic Press, Hudson 1995.
The Effects of Esoteric Development (GA 145) [The Hague 1913]. Anthroposophic Press, Hudson 1997.
Festivals and their Meaning [29 lectures, various venues, between 1907 and 1923]. Rudolf Steiner Press, London 1996.
The Spiritual Hierarchies and the Physical World (GA 110) [Düsseldorf 1909]. Anthroposophic Press, Hudson 1996.

World History and the Mysteries in the Light of Anthroposophy (GA 233) [Dornach 1923/4]. Rudolf Steiner Press, London 1997.

Reincarnation and Karma (GA 135) [Berlin & Stuttgart 1912]. Steiner Book Centre, Toronto 1977.

Introducing Anthroposophical Medicine (GA 312) [Dornach 1920]. Anthroposophic Press, Hudson 1999.

Psychoanalysis and Spiritual Psychology (GA 178, 143, 205) [Dornach & Munich 1912–1921]. Anthroposophic Press, Hudson 1990.

Education of the Child and Early Lectures on Education [various venues, 1906–1911]. Anthroposophic Press, Hudson 1996.

The Child's Changing Consciousness and Waldorf Education (GA 306) [Dornach 1923]. Anthroposophic Press & Rudolf Steiner Press, New York & London 1988.

The Kingdom of Childhood (GA 311) [Torquay 1924]. Anthroposophic Press, Hudson 1995.

Education for Special Needs (GA 317) [Dornach 1924]. Rudolf Steiner Press, London 1998.

World Economy (GA 340) [Dornach 1922]. Rudolf Steiner Press, London 1977.

Agriculture (GA 327) [Koberwitz 1924]. Bio-Dynamic Farming & Gardening Association Inc., Kimberton 1993.

Anthroposophy and Science (GA 324) [Stuttgart 1921]. Mercury Press, Spring Valley 1991.

Boundaries of Natural Science (GA 322) [Dornach 1920]. Anthroposophic Press, New York 1983.

Architecture as a Synthesis of the Arts (GA 286) [various venues, 1911–1924]. Rudolf Steiner Press, London 1999.

Colour (GA 291) [Dornach 1914–1924]. Rudolf Steiner Press, London 1996.

Introduction to Eurythmy (GA 277a) [various venues, 1913–1924]. Anthroposophic Press, New York 1984.

The Inner Nature of Music and the Experience of Tone (GA 283) [various venues, 1906–1923]. Anthroposophic Press, New York 1983.

Books on Rudolf Steiner by Other Authors

Biographies:
H. Barnes, *A Life for the Spirit, Rudolf Steiner in the Crosscurrents of Our Time*, Anthroposophic Press, New York 1997.
S. C. Easton, *Rudolf Steiner, Herald of a New Epoch*, Anthroposophic Press, New York 1980.
G. Childs, *Rudolf Steiner, His Life and Work, An Illustrated Biography*, Floris Books, Edinburgh 1995.

On his core teaching:
S. O. Prokofieff, *Rudolf Steiner and the Founding of the New Mysteries*, Temple Lodge Publishing, London 1994.
R. Wilkinson, *Rudolf Steiner, Aspects of his Spiritual World-View, Anthroposophy*, Volumes 1, 2 & 3, Temple Lodge Publishing, London 1993/4.
B. Nesfield-Cookson, *Rudolf Steiner's Vision of Love*, Rudolf Steiner Press, London 1999.

On practical initiatives:
W. Schilthuis, *Biodynamic Agriculture*, Floris Books, Edinburgh 1994.
M. Luxford, *Children with Special Needs*, Floris Books, Edinburgh 1994.
T. Poplawski, *Eurythmy, Rhythm, Dance and Soul*, Floris Books, Edinburgh 1998.
K. Bayes, *Living Architecture*, Floris Books, Edinburgh 1994.
Rev. J. H. Hindes, *Renewing Christianity*, Floris Books, Edinburgh 1995.
C. Clouder, M. Rawson, *Waldorf Education*, Floris Books, Edinburgh 1998.

INDEX OF NAMES

(Italic page numbers refer to pictures)

For the signatories to the 'Appeal to the German People', see p.138–9.